Nurturing Character in the Classroom

Ethical Action

EthEx Series Book 4

Nurturing Character in the Classroom, EthEx Series

Ethical Sensitivity
Ethical Judgment
Ethical Motivation
Ethical Action

CURRICULUM & COURSE-BASED TEXTS & RESOURCES DIVISION

Alliance for Catholic Education Press
at the University of Notre Dame

Nurturing Character in the Classroom
Ethical Action
EthEx Series Book 4

Darcia Narvaez, Ph.D.

ALLIANCE FOR CATHOLIC EDUCATION PRESS
AT THE UNIVERSITY OF NOTRE DAME

Notre Dame, Indiana

Alliance for Catholic Education Press
at the University of Notre Dame
158 IEI Building
Notre Dame, IN 46556
http://www.nd.edu/~acepress

Text design by Tonia Bock
Cover design by Mary Jo Adams Kocovski

ISBN: 978-0-9819501-3-6

Library of Congress Cataloging-in-Publication Data

Narvaez, Darcia.
  Ethical action / Darcia Narvaez.
     p. cm. -- (Nurturing character in the classroom, EthEx series ; v. bk 4)
  Includes bibliographical references and index.
  Summary: "Provides a framework and instructional materials for integrating ethical education, specifically ethical action, into the middle school classroom and curriculum"--Provided by publisher.
  ISBN 978-0-9819501-3-6 (pbk. : alk. paper)
 1. Moral education (Middle school)--United States. 2. Ethics--Study and teaching (Middle school)--United States. I. Title.

  LC268.N237 2009
  372.01'14--dc22
                                        2009005566

This book was printed on acid-free paper.

Printed in the United States of America.

Table of Contents

Foreword

For the past several years my colleagues and I at the University of Minnesota, in partnership with the Minnesota Department of Children, Families and Learning, have been developing a model for character education in the middle grades that we call "Community Voices and Character Education." Here are the six key characteristics of our model.

First, we adopt a skills-based understanding of moral character. This is not a new idea. Plato believed that the just person is like an artisan who has particular, highly-cultivated skills that have been developed through training and practice (Plato, 1987). Persons of good character, then, have better developed skills in four areas: ethical sensitivity, ethical judgment, ethical motivation, and ethical action (Narvaez, Mitchell, Endicott, & Bock, 1999). For example, experts in the skills of Ethical Sensitivity are better at quickly and accurately "reading" a moral situation and determining what role they might play (Narvaez & Endicott, 2009). Experts in the skills of Ethical Judgment have many tools for solving complex moral problems (Narvaez & Bock, 2009). Experts in the skills of Ethical Motivation cultivate an ethical identity that leads them to prioritize ethical goals (Narvaez & Lies, 2009). Experts in the skills of Ethical Action know how to keep their "eye on the prize," enabling them to stay on task and take the necessary steps to get the ethical job done (Narvaez, 2009). Our approach to character development, then, insists on a holistic understanding of the moral person (Narvaez, Bock, & Endicott, 2003). It views character as a set of component skills that can be cultivated to high levels of expertise.

Expertise is a notion that has gained prominence among educational researchers (e.g., Sternberg, 1998, 1999). According to this view, children move along a continuum from novice-to-expert in each content domain that they study. Unlike novices, experts have larger, more complex and better organized knowledge (Chi, Glaser, & Farr, 1988; Sternberg, 1998). Experts see the world differently (Neisser, 1967). Their extensive pattern matching capabilities allow experts to notice things that novices miss (Novick, 1988). Experts possess well-developed sets of procedural skills. Unlike novices, experts know *what* knowledge to access, *which* procedures to apply, *how* to apply them, and *when* it is appropriate (Abernathy & Hamm, 1995; Hogarth, 2001).

Second, to help children develop character skills in the way that experts do, we adopt a scientifically-based, cognitive approach to learning and teaching that assumes that children actively construct representations of the world (Narvaez, 2002; Piaget, 1932/1965, 1952, 1970). Best practice instruction provides opportunities for students to develop more accurate and better organized representations and the procedural skills required to use them (Anderson, 1989). Like the expert, students learn to master the defining features and underlying structures of a domain through practice that is focused, extensive, and coached (Ericsson & Charness, 1994; Ericsson, Krampe, & Tesch-Roemer, 1993). The educator provides authentic learning experiences that are structured according to what we know about levels of apprenticeship (Marshall, 1995; Rogoff, Baker-Sennett, Lacasa, & Goldsmith, 1995).

Third, our model insists that character development be embedded within standards-driven academic instruction, for ultimately this is the only way character education will be sustained.

Fourth, character should be taught across the curriculum in every subject and activity, for character skills are required not in isolation but throughout every encounter in life.

Fifth, our model opens character education to greater accountability, in the sense that skills are teachable and progress toward mastery can be measured.

Sixth, a curricular approach to character education must be an intentional collaboration with "community voices." After all, students are apprentices to the community. The issue of "whose values will be taught?" is best approached by embedding educational goals within the value commitments of particular communities.

Does this model work? Our preliminary data are quite promising. For example, classrooms using our approach showed increases in scores on prosocial responsibility, ethical identity, and prosocial risk-taking, while a comparison group did not.

In summary, moral character is best thought of as a set of teachable, ethically-relevant skills. Ethical skill instruction should be embedded in standards-driven pedagogy. Ethical skills should be taught across the curriculum and cultivated by community voices. With such an education, students will develop schemas of goodness and of justice. They will learn routines of helping and of reasoning. They will learn skills of leadership and of commitment. With these skills they can take responsibility for ethical action in their neighborhoods and in their communities. They will be energized by memories of personal ethical action. With these skills, students are empowered to be active citizens who will make the fate of the nation their own.

Speech at the Whitehouse Conference on Character and Community
Darcia Narvaez, Ph.D.
Associate Professor, University of Notre Dame
June 2002

References

Abernathy, C. M., & Hamm, R. M. (1995). *Surgical intuition*. Philadelphia: Hanley & Belfus.

Anderson, L. M. (1989). Learners and learning. In M. C. Reynolds (Ed.), *Knowledge base for the beginning teacher* (pp. 85-99). Oxford: Pergamon Press.

Chi, M. T. H., Glaser, R., & Farr, M. (1988*). The nature of expertise*. Hillsdale, NJ: Erlbaum.

Ericsson, K. A., & Charness, N. (1994). Expert performance: Its structure and acquisition. *American Psychologist, 49*, 725-747.

Ericsson, K. A., Krampe, R. T., & Tesch-Roemer, C. (1993). The role of deliberate practice in the acquisition of expert performance. *Psychological Review, 100*(3), 363-406.

Hogarth, R. M. (2001). *Educating intuition*. Chicago: University of Chicago Press.

Marshall, S. P. (1995). *Schemas in problem solving*. Cambridge: Cambridge University Press.

Narvaez, D. (2002). Does reading moral stories build character? *Educational Psychology Review, 14*(2), 155-171.

Narvaez, D. (2009). *Ethical action: Nurturing character in the classroom, EthEx Series, Book 4*. Notre Dame, IN: Alliance for Catholic Education Press.

Narvaez, D., & Bock, T. (2009). *Ethical judgment: Nurturing character in the classroom, EthEx Series, Book 2*. Notre Dame, IN: Alliance for Catholic Education Press.

Narvaez, D., Bock, T., & Endicott, L. (2003). Who should I become? Citizenship, goodness, moral flourishing, and ethical expertise. In W. Veugelers & F. Oser (Eds.), *Teaching in moral and democratic education*. Bern: P. Lang.

Narvaez, D., & Endicott, L. (2009). *Ethical sensitivity: Nurturing character in the classroom, EthEx Series, Book 1*. Notre Dame, IN: Alliance for Catholic Education Press.

Narvaez, D., & Lies, J. (2009). *Ethical motivation: Nurturing character in the classroom, EthEx Series, Book 3*. Notre Dame, IN: Alliance for Catholic Education Press.

Narvaez, D., Mitchell, C., Endicott, L., & Bock, T. (1999). *Nurturing character in the middle school classroom: A guidebook for teachers*. St. Paul, MN: Department of Children, Families, and Learning.

Neisser, U. (1967). *Cognitive psychology*. New York: Appletown-Century-Crofts.

Novick, L. R. (1988). Analogical transfer, problem similarity, and expertise. *Journal of Experimental Psychology: Learning, Memory, & Cognition, 14*(3), 510-520.

Piaget, J. (1952). *The origin of intelligence in children*. New York: International University Press.

Piaget, J. (1965*). The moral judgment of the child* (M. Gabain, Trans.). New York: Free Press. (Original work published 1932)

Piaget, J. (1970). *Genetic epistemology* (E. Duckworth, Trans.). New York: Columbia University Press.

Plato. (1987). *The republic*. London: Penguin.

Rogoff, B., Baker-Sennett, J., Lacasa, P., & Goldsmith, D. (1995). Development through participation in sociocultural activity. *Cultural Practices as Contexts for Development: New Directions for Child and Adolescent Development, 67*, 45-64.

Sternberg, R. (1998). Abilities are forms of developing expertise. *Educational Researcher, 3*, 22-35.

Sternberg, R. (1999). Intelligence as developing expertise. *Contemporary Educational Psychology, 24*(4), 359-375.

Preface

The *Nurturing Character in the Classroom, EthEx Series* materials were developed under the auspices of the Minnesota Community Voices and Character Education project (grant# R215V980001 from the U. S. Department of Education Office of Educational Research and Improvement to the Minnesota Department of Children, Families and Learning during 1998-2002).

The *Nurturing Character in the Classroom, EthEx Series* materials were developed in collaboration with teachers across the state of Minnesota and were tested throughout the project by volunteer teams of educators. **For a report of the final-year evaluation, see Narvaez, Bock, Endicott, and Lies (2004).**

EthEx refers to the lifelong development of ethical skills toward expertise (**eth**ical **ex**pertise) in many domains and situations. The four EthEx books (sensitivity, judgment, motivation, action) suggest skills and subskills required for virtuous life. The books also lay out how to teach them through four levels of expertise development.

EthEx is incorporated into the **Integrative Ethical Education** model (Narvaez, 2006, 2007, 2008, in press). The Integrative Ethical Education model has five steps for educators including (along with EthEx) the importance of a caring relationship with each student, a supportive climate (for achievement and character), student self-regulation for character and achievement, and restoring community networks and support.

These booklets were developed for the middle school level (ages 11-15), but elementary and high school teachers have used them successfully as well.

For **staff development** in your school, please contact Darcia Narvaez at the University of Notre Dame, Department of Psychology (dnarvaez@nd.edu). For questions or other materials, also contact Dr. Narvaez.

References

Narvaez, D. (2006). Integrative ethical education. In M. Killen & J. Smetana (Eds.), *Handbook of moral development* (pp. 703-733). Mahwah, NJ: Erlbaum.

Narvaez, D. (2007). How cognitive and neurobiological sciences inform values education for creatures like us. In D. Aspin & J. Chapman (Eds.), *Values education and lifelong learning: Philosophy, policy, practices* (pp. 127-159). Dordrecht, The Netherlands: Springer Press International.

Narvaez, D. (2008). Human flourishing and moral development: Cognitive science and neurobiological perspectives on virtue development. In L. Nucci & D. Narvaez (Eds.), *Handbook of moral and character education* (pp. 310-327). New York: Routledge.

Narvaez, D. (in press). *Moral development: A pragmatic approach to fostering engagement and imagination.*

Narvaez, D., Bock, T., Endicott, L., & Lies, J. (2004). Minnesota's voices and character education project. *Journal of Research in Character Education, 2,* 89-112.

Acknowledgments

Thanks to former University of Minnesota Team Members and affiliates whose ideas or efforts were influential at one point or another in the development of materials: Christyan Mitchell, Jolynn Gardner, Ruth Schiller, and Laura Staples.

Thanks to Connie Anderson, Minnesota Department of Children, Families and Learning, for her wisdom and leadership throughout the Community Voices and Character Education Project.

Special thanks to our school-based collaborators from across the state of Minnesota who kept us focused on what really works and what really helps the classroom teacher.

Introduction
to the
Ethical Expertise Model
(EthEx)

Purpose and Goals of the EthEx Model

At the beginning of the 21st century, children are less likely to spend time under adult supervision than they were in the past. As a result, children's ethical education has become haphazard, and subject to strong influence from popular media. To help the development of children, we seek to assist educators develop curricula that teach character while simultaneously meeting regular academic requirements. We apply research-based theory to instruction for ethical development, using an expertise model of ethical behavior that is based on research and applied to ethics education.

The Four Guide Books for Teachers

We have created four books[1] that address the four main psychological processes involved in behaving ethically: Ethical Sensitivity, Ethical Judgment, Ethical Motivation, and Ethical Action. Each book provides suggestions for ways to work on the skills of the process within regular lessons. Each book links ethics education to regular academic requirements. The four books are designed to help teachers develop a conscious and conscientious approach to helping students build character.

Why Not a Curriculum?

There are several problems with set curricula. First, the lessons are written out of the context of the classroom for which they are designed to be used. Consequently, no pre-fabricated lesson is actually taught exactly as designed because the teacher must adapt it to the students and class at hand. Second, we have seen too many curricula used once or twice and set aside as other demands claim teacher attention. So, although a set curriculum may appear more useful to the teacher at the outset, in the end it can become "old" as the latest mandate takes precedence. Third, an outside, packaged curriculum is often not assimilated into the teacher's way of thinking about instruction. Hence, it may feel "alien" to the teacher, a feeling that is correspondingly felt by students. So we believe that the best way to change teaching over the long term is to help teachers modify what they already teach. We make suggestions for changes, but the teacher herself modifies lessons in ways that work for her and her students. We believe that teacher tailoring is an approach that can bring lasting change.

[1]These materials have been developed under the auspices of grant # R215V980001 from the U.S. Department of Education Office of Educational Research and Improvement.

Should Teachers Teach Values?
They already are

To educate a person in mind and not in morals is to educate a menace to society.
-Theodore Roosevelt

The United States at the beginning of the 21st century has reached a new pinnacle. There is more prosperity throughout the society than ever before. There are more equal rights across groups (e.g., males and females, minorities and majorities) than at any time in the history of the world. There are comforts U.S. citizens enjoy that are accessible only to the wealthy in many other nations of the world (e.g., clean water, sewage, inexpensive clothes, and food). Then why are children around the nation shooting their peers at school? Why do so many lament our public behavior and sense of community? Why do some argue that our social supports are the worst among industrialized countries of the world (e.g., no national day care, few national benefits for parents)? Why does the U.S. have a greater percentage of its citizens imprisoned than any other nation save Russia? Certainly there are multiple causes for these outcomes. Many people, however, are concerned about the cultural health of our nation.

What do you think of our nation's cultural health? Take, for example, current standards for public behavior—are they better or worse than in the past? What do you think of popular culture? Television shows use language, discuss topics, and show interactions that would not have been broached just a few years ago. For the sake of entertainment, committed couples allow themselves to be placed on "Temptation Island" in order to test how committed they really are. Is that all right? On the popular show "The Ozbournes" the parents fully use profanity. Does it matter? Professional athletes can be felons and still receive acclaim from fans and the news media. Should we care? Many have noted that citizens are increasingly impatient, self-absorbed, and rude in public. Have you noticed? Most notably, people are harming and killing others over traffic offenses (e.g., Road Rage Summit, Minneapolis, April 29, 1999).

Citizens of other industrialized nations are appalled by our culture and consider us a nation of self-indulgent adolescents:

> Americans are like children: noisy, curious, unable to keep a secret, not given
> to subtlety, and prone to misbehave in public. Once one accepts the American's
> basically adolescent nature, the rest of their culture falls into place and what at
> first seemed thoughtless and silly appears charming and energetic. (Faul, 1994,
> p. 5)

Do you agree? Do you believe that individuals in the United States overemphasize their rights with little thought for their responsibilities to others? Do they (we) overemphasize individualism at the expense of collective goals as communitarians contend (e.g., Bellah, Madsen, Sullivan, Swidler, & Tipton, 1985; Etzioni, 1994)? According to this perspective, everyone is rushing from one activity to another with little thought for neighbors. The patience that is learned from long-time interaction with neighbors is not being fostered. Instead, impatience with others seems the norm. Miss Manners concurs, believing that we have a civility crisis.

Consider today's families. At the dawn of the 21st century in the United States, it is normal for parents (supported by corresponding laws and social beliefs) to think of themselves as individuals first and family members second, making it easy to divorce a spouse even when there are children. Even as a single parent works hard to support the family (or both parents work to maintain a standard of living formerly supported by one income), many are unable to provide the support and supervision their children need (Steinberg, 1996). As a result, children are not getting enough adult attention. A third of them are depressed. Too many commit suicide. They turn to their peers for values, support, and goals.[2] Children spend more time with television, with all its contemporary crudities, than with their parents. Children's values are cultivated willy-nilly by their daily experience largely apart from adults. Some young people admire Eminem, a White rap singer whose songs are replete with the raping or killing of women (including his mother). In fact, some sociologists and philosophers have suggested that U.S. culture, in its fascination with killing, is a culture not only of violence but of death. Such are the values that children bring to school.

"So what?" you might say. "I try not to make judgments about the cultures of my students. I let the students make up their own minds. I don't teach values in my classroom." Really? Is any behavior acceptable in your room? If not, you are teaching values; you are indicating that some behaviors are better than others. Not hitting is better than hitting. Not cheating is better than cheating. On a daily basis, you decide which students or behaviors get rewarded and which get punished. Teachers make decisions about how "the benefits and burdens of living together are distributed" (Rest, 1986). Teachers decide how to manage the competition and cooperation that humans bring to social interactions. In short, teachers are teaching values all day long.

[2] Unlike most other industrialized nations, there are few social supports outside the home that are built into our system; it was designed to rely on the strength of the nuclear family and extended family. A high rate of single parenting, both parents working and the resultant guilt, lack of parenting skills, lack of extended family support, and a cultural milieu oriented to pleasure rather than self-sacrifice all contribute to the decline in communal satisfaction. Instead of child raising being shared across society, the schools are shouldering the many needs that growing (and neglected or abused) children have.

Teachers' Ethical Decisions

We urge teachers to be both conscious of and conscientious about the values they are teaching.

There are many morally-relevant situations in schools in which teachers make decisions that affect student welfare. Here are a few concrete examples of value teaching:

- When teachers **divide the class into groups**, they are conveying what should be noticed (e.g., gender) and what they value (e.g., cooperation, achievement). By doing this they reinforce what students should notice and value.
- When teachers **discipline** students, the students learn what behaviors are important in that classroom (or in the hallway, depending on where the disciplining takes place).
- The **school rules the teacher enforces (or doesn't enforce)** reveal how seriously the students should take rules in school and in general.
- The **standards a teacher applies** to behavior, homework, and attitudes are practiced (and learned) by the students in the classroom.
- **The way a classroom is structured physically** and the way the teacher sets up procedures (and which ones) demonstrate the values held by the teacher. For example, if the teacher wants to emphasize creativity he or she may have colorful decor, alternating seating arrangements, and may allow freedom of choice in selecting academic activities.
- **The teacher's communication style** (quiet and firm, or playful and easy going) can set the climate and convey expectations for behavior.
- Whether or not and how teachers **communicate with parents** show how parents are valued.
- **Grading policies** are another way that teachers distribute the benefits and burdens available in the classroom—does the teacher use norm-references or criterion-references or contract-based grading?
- **Curriculum content selection** can convey a high regard for one culture over another, one viewpoint over another. Whether or not teachers assign homework over religious holidays (and whose holidays) reveal the teacher's expectations and values.
- **The teacher's cultural assumptions** about the social context and his or her instinctive responses to students convey non-verbally who is valued and who is not. This may be one of the most important features of a classroom for a minority student whose success may be at risk.

In short, teachers teach values whether or not they realize it. We urge teachers to be both conscious and conscientious about the values they are teaching. Hence this book has goals for teacher development. As teachers develop curricula using our principles, they will learn the principles to use in their professional behavior. First, we will discuss the process of ethical behavior. Then we will discuss how to apply this knowledge in the classroom—for both curriculum and for general climate in the classroom. Based on these materials, teachers will be able to design activities and a classroom that promote ethical behavior.

This is not to say that teachers currently are without guidance as to promoting an ethical classroom. Teachers have a code of ethics to which they subscribe when obtaining a license and a position. Notice the table from the National Education Association's Code of Ethics. These codes affect much of what teachers decide and do. Notice that the NEA code is not one of "doing no harm," but is proactive, that is, "doing good."

FROM THE CODE OF ETHICS OF THE EDUCATION PROFESSION
(National Education Association, 1975)

Principle 1: Commitment to the student.

In fulfillment to the student, the educator

1. Shall not unreasonably restrain the student from independent action in the pursuit of learning.
2. Shall not unreasonably deny the student access to varying points of view.
3. Shall not deliberately suppress or distort subject matter relevant to the student's progress.
4. Shall make reasonable effort to protect the student from conditions harmful to learning or to health and safety.
5. Shall not intentionally expose the student to embarrassment or disparagement.
6. Shall not on the basis of race, color, creed, sex, national origin, marital status, political or religious beliefs, family, social or cultural background, or sexual orientation, unfairly:
    a. Exclude any student from participation in any program;
    b. Deny benefits to any student;
    c. Grant any advantage to any student.

The NEA code requires teachers:

* to present more than one viewpoint,
* to present the full gamut of subject matter relevant to the student,
* to protect the student from harm.

These are actions that require conscious deliberation. For example, questions the teacher might consider are: What are multiple viewpoints on this topic? What content should be included? What harms students and how can I design an environment and classroom atmosphere that is least harmful? What if a student has a viewpoint that is legitimately harmful or wrong? If the teacher does not deliberately plan around these issues, chances are there will be only mainstream viewpoints presented, the subject matter will be narrow, and the student may have to tolerate insults and other harm from peers.

We believe that there is more to ethical education than even following a code of ethics. The code provides a minimal set of general guidelines. Promoting ethical behavior in students requires not only a deliberate effort but a theory for what ethical behavior entails. In character education programs across the country, it is not always clear what direction these efforts should take. That is the topic of the next section.

What Should Be Taught?
The Process Model of Ethical Behavior

When a curriculum claims to be educating for character, what should it mean? What are the aspects of ethics that should be addressed? As a framework for analysis, we use the process model of ethical behavior as described by Rest (1983) and advocated by Bebeau, Rest, and Narvaez (1999). The model includes ethical sensitivity, ethical judgment, ethical motivation, and ethical action. See the framework outlined below and described in the next section.

The Process Model of Ethical Behavior

ETHICAL SENSITIVITY
NOTICE!
Pick up on the cues related to
ethical decision making and behavior;
Interpret the situation according to who is involved,
what actions to take, and what possible reactions
and outcomes might ensue.

ETHICAL JUDGMENT
THINK!
Reason about the possible actions in the situation
and judge which action is most ethical.

ETHICAL MOTIVATION
AIM!
Prioritize the ethical action over other goals and needs
(either in the particular situation, or as a habit).

ETHICAL ACTION
ACT!
Implement the ethical action by knowing how to do so
and follow through despite hardship

How the Ethical Process Model Works

A kindergarten student in New York City dies midyear from longstanding child abuse at the hands of a parent. The community is shocked that the teacher and school did not prevent the untimely death.

The star of the boy's basketball team is flunking English. If he gets a failing grade, he won't be able to play on the team. Should the teacher give him a passing grade so that the team has a chance to win the championship and boost school morale?

An American Indian student won't look the teacher in the eye nor volunteer answers in class. How should the teacher respond?

From large effects to small, the ethical behavior of teachers—or the lack thereof—influences children's lives on a daily basis (e.g., Bergem, 1990; Goodlad, Soder, & Sirotnik, 1990). Decisions about grading and grouping; decisions about curriculum, instructional style, assessment; decisions about the allotment of time, care, and encouragement (which students, when, where, and how?)—all of these are ethical decisions the educator faces each day. How can teachers sort out the processes of ethical decision making?

First, one must know what ethical behavior looks like. When thinking about ethical behavior, it is often helpful to think of ethical failure. For example, albeit an extreme one, think of the teacher whose student dies from child abuse. How is it that the teacher did not take ethical action and intervene? There are many points at which failure might have occurred. First, the teacher would have to recognize the signs and symptoms of abuse, and have some empathic reaction to the child's circumstance. Having noticed and felt concern, the teacher would need to think about what action might be taken and what outcomes might occur. Then the teacher must reason about the choices and decide which action to take. (In order for ethical behavior to eventually occur, the teacher would need to select an ethical action). Next, the teacher would need to prioritize the chosen (ethical) action over other needs, motives, and goals. Finally, the teacher would need to know what steps to take to implement the decision, and persevere until the action was completed. It is apparent that there are a lot of places where things can go wrong. For example, the teacher may not see the signs or may make a bad judgment or may have other priorities or may not know what to do or may give up in frustration. In effect, ethical failure can stem from any one or more of these weaknesses.

Rest (1983) has asked: What psychological elements are involved in bringing about an ethical action? He has suggested that there are at least four psychological processes of ethical behavior that must occur in order for an ethical behavior to ensue. These four processes are:

(1) *Ethical Sensitivity:* Noticing the cues that indicate a moral situation is at hand. Identifying the persons who are interested in possible actions and outcomes and how the interested parties might respond to the range of possible actions and outcomes.

(2) *Ethical Judgment:* Making a decision about what is ethically right or ethically wrong in the situation.

(3) *Ethical Motivation:* Placing the ethical action choice at the top of one's priorities, over all other personal values at the moment.

(4) *Ethical Action:* Having the necessary ego strength and implementation skills to complete the action despite obstacles, opposition, and fatigue.

In an effort to make these processes clear, let us look at a specific situation in a classroom to which we will apply the processes. Let us imagine that Mr. Anderson has a classroom of children in which Abraham is hitting Maria. Now let us look at each of the processes in relation to this event.

Process 1: Ethical Sensitivity

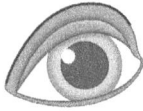

Picking up on the cues related to ethical decision making and ethical behavior.
Interpreting the situation according to who is involved,
what actions to take, what possible reactions and outcomes might ensue.

Teachers need to be able to detect and interpret environmental cues correctly in order for the other processes of ethical behavior to be initiated. For example, if Mr. Anderson completely fails to see Abraham hitting Maria, there will be no consideration of action choices or action taken. In order to perceive the action, such an occurrence must be salient because, for example, it is unusual. On the other hand, Mr. Anderson may not notice the hitting if it is a daily class-wide event, or if it is an agreed-upon sign of affection.

Ethical Sensitivity

Notice a problem (sensibilities)
What kinds of problems are salient to me, my family, my community, my affiliative groups?

State the situation (critical thinking)
What is the problem? How did the problem come about? How much time is there to make a decision? How does my community identify the problem? How do elders in my family identify the problem? How does my religion or family culture affect my perceptions?

State the interested parties (critical thinking)
Who are the people who will be affected by this decision (family, community, affiliative groups)? Who should be consulted in this decision? Who has faced this problem before? With whom could I talk about the problem?

Weigh the possible outcomes—short-term and long-term (creative thinking)
What are the possible consequences to me, my family/community/affiliative groups for each possible action? What are the possible reactions of these interested parties? What are the potential benefits for me, my family/community/affinity groups for each possible action? Who else might be affected? How will my choice affect the rest of the world now and in the future?

List all possible options (creative thinking)
How could the problem be solved? What are the choices I have for solving the problem? How would my community/family/cultural group solve the problem? What are the choices my family/cultural/community allow? Should I consider other options?

In intercultural/intersocial-class situations, cue misperception may take place, leading to improper action or no action at all. For example, a middle-class teacher in the U.S.A. may subconsciously perceive the downcast eyes of a Native American student in conversation with her as a sign of disrespect toward her authority. But in the student's own culture, the opposite is the case. However, out of ignorance the teacher may take an action to re-establish her authority, for example, punish the child. In contrast, a child may exhibit disrespectful behavior for his own subculture, such as severe slouching for some African-American communities.

However, this action is not really noticed since it is not considered out of the or-dinary by the non-African-American teacher or interpreted as a threat to her au-thority (which it is intended to be) but is considered to be an acceptable expres-sion of frustration on behalf of the student. In this case, the teacher interprets (subconsciously) the child's behavior as a personal freedom issue rather than the challenge to authority (a responsibility issue) that it is.

Ethical sensitivity includes subconscious processing which is often culturally based. As such, teachers need to become aware of their culturally-based expecta-tions and to broaden their understanding of other cultural perspectives in order to circumvent misinterpretation of student behavior.

Not only is Mr. Anderson faced with many perceptual cues to sort through each day, he is also faced with countless situations in which he must make decisions with partial information. Before making a decision, he must interpret situations contextually, according to who is interested in the outcome, what actions and outcomes are possible and how the interested people might react to each. Many problems are much more complicated than in our example (e.g., whether or not to promote a student to the next grade). Here, it is obvious that hitting is generally wrong.

In our incident with Abraham and Maria, Mr. Anderson has noticed the action and finds it out of the ordinary and unacceptable. Now he must determine who is interested in the decision he makes about the incident—certainly Abraham and Maria would be interested, as well as their parents and families, the school admin-istrator, not to speak of the other children in the classroom. Next, he thinks about the actions he could take in this situation and the likely outcomes and reactions of interested parties. For example, he might quickly think:

> Well, I could stop what I am doing and verbally intervene in front of the whole
> class. Maybe that is not such a good idea because it would disrupt everyone's work.
> If Abraham does not stop, other children might notice and perhaps think that
> hitting was permissible. I could walk over there and physically intervene—grab
> Abraham's hand. That would stop it and still draw attention from the others—
> maybe they would learn something. Or, I could ignore it, since Abraham tends to do
> this when he gets excited—he means no harm. But how would Maria react to
> that? If I don't do something, Maria's parents might complain to the administrator.

Ethical sensitivity involves attending to relevant events and mapping out pos-sible actions and their effects. It includes a subtle interaction between both conscious and subconscious processing.

ETHICAL SENSITIVITY SKILLS	
ES-1: Understanding Emotional Expression	ES-4: Responding to Diversity
ES-2: Taking the Perspective of Others	ES-5: Controlling Social Bias
ES-3: Connecting to Others	ES-6: Interpreting Situations
	ES-7: Communicating Well

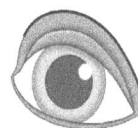

Intro to the EthEx Model

Process 2: Ethical Judgment

*Reasoning about the possible actions in the situation
and judging which action is most ethical.*

Following this exploration of possible actions and reactions, the ethical actor must decide on which course of action to take. Ethical judgment is the process of making a decision about which action of all the options is the most moral action. Lawrence Kohlberg (1984) defined different ways that people make decisions about how to get along with others (see the chart on p. 15). Whereas in ethical sensitivity, cultural differences are particularly important, in moral judgment, normative developmental trends in moral judgment are important. The types of moral reasoning Kohlberg found are developmental and have been identified in dozens of countries around the world. Although there are other types of criteria individuals use to make ethical decisions, Kohlberg's framework has extensive empirical research support. In addition, the vast majority of research shows no gender differences.

Ethical Judgment

Make a decision
What is the best action to take? What choice should I make? Why?

Ethical judgment concerns choosing the ethical action from the choices considered in the process of ethical sensitivity; this decision will be influenced by the ethical reasoning structures of the decision maker. In other words, Mr. Anderson selects the action that is the most ethical in the particular situation according to his level of ethical judgment development. In our scenario, Mr. Anderson may decide that, out of the choices we listed above, going over to Abraham and physically intervening is the most defensible ethical action:

It prevents further harm to Maria, and has ramifications for future behavior by Abraham and the rest of the class. It sends a clear signal both to Abraham and the rest of the class about how the students should NOT treat each other. I can use it as an opportunity to discuss the importance of following rules to keep order and safety in the classroom.

ETHICAL JUDGMENT SKILLS
EJ-1: Reasoning Generally
EJ-2: Reasoning Ethically
EJ-3: Understanding Ethical Problems
EJ-4: Using Codes and Identifying Judgment Criteria
EJ-5: Understanding Consequences
EJ-6: Reflecting on the Process and Outcome
EJ-7: Coping

Intro to the EthEx Model

SIX CONCEPTUAL STAGES ABOUT COOPERATION AND THEIR CHARACTERISTICS
(From Rest, 1979)

PRECONVENTIONAL LEVEL

Stage 1: The ethicality of obedience: Do what you are told.
- Right and wrong are defined simply in terms of obedience to fixed rules.
- Punishment inevitably follows disobedience, and anyone who is punished must have been bad.
Example: Follow class rules to avoid detention.

Stage 2: The ethicality of instrumental egoism: Let's make a deal.
- An act is right if it serves an individual's desires and interests.
- One should obey the law only if it is prudent to do so.
- Cooperative interaction is based on simple exchange.
Example: Do chores to get allowance.

CONVENTIONAL LEVEL

Stage 3: The ethicality of interpersonal concordance: Be considerate, nice and kind, and you'll make friends.
- An act is good if it is based on a prosocial motive.
- Being ethical implies concern for the other's approval.
Example: Share your gum with the class and people will find you likeable.

Stage 4: The ethicality of law and duty to the social order: Everyone in society is obligated to and protected by the law.
- Right is defined by categorical rules, binding on all, that fix shared expectations, thereby providing a basis for social order.
- Values are derived from and subordinated to the social order and maintenance of law.
- Respect for delegated authority is part of one's obligations to society.
Example: Obey traffic lights because it's the law.

POSTCONVENTIONAL

Stage 5: The ethicality of consensus-building procedures: You are obligated by the arrangements that are agreed to by due process procedures.
- Ethical obligation derives from voluntary commitments of society's members to cooperate.
- Procedures exist for selecting laws that maximize welfare as discerned in the majority will.
- Basic rights are preconditions to social obligations.
Example: Obey traffic lights because they are designed to keep us all safe.

Stage 6: The ethicality of non-arbitrary social cooperation: How rational and impartial people would organize cooperation defines ethicality.
- Ethical judgments are ultimately justified by principles of ideal cooperation.
- Individuals each have an equal claim to benefit from the governing principles of cooperation.
Example: Everyone agrees that traffic lights keep us safe and so they will obey them for the common good.

Process 3: Ethical Motivation

*Prioritizing the ethical action over other goals and needs
(either in the particular situation, or as a habit).*

Following Mr. Anderson's decision about which action is most ethical, he must be motivated to prioritize that action, that is, be ethically motivated. Ethical motivation can be viewed in two ways, as situation-specific and as situation-general. Situation-general motivation concerns the day-to-day attitudes about getting along with others. It is a positive attitude towards ethical action that one maintains day to day. Blasi (1984) and Damon (1984) argue that self-concept has a great deal to do with ethical motivation generally, including attending to professional ethical codes. For instance, if one has a concept that one is an ethical person, one is more likely to prioritize ethical behaviors. Situation-specific ethical motivation concerns the prioritization of the ethical action choice in a particular situation. If all goes well, matching one's professional and personal priorities with possible actions results in ethical motivation, prioritizing the ethical action.

Ethical Motivation

Value identification
What are the values of my family/religion/culture/community? How should these values influence what is decided? How does each possible option fit with these values?

Prioritize the action
Am I willing to forego the benefits of NOT taking this best action?

Ethical motivation means that the person has placed the ethical course of action—which was selected in the process of ethical judgment— at the top of the list of action priorities. In other words, all other competing actions, values and concerns are set aside so that the ethical action can be completed. In other words, does a teacher put aside another priority at the moment, such as taking a break, in order to take an ethical action, such as stopping one student from insulting another? In our situation with Mr. Anderson, in order to continue along the route to completing an ethical action, he would have to put aside any other priority (such as teaching the lesson) and focus on performing the ethical action.

ETHICAL MOTIVATION SKILLS	
EM-1: Respecting Others	EM-4: Being a Community Member
EM-2: Cultivating Conscience	EM-5: Finding Meaning in Life
EM-3: Acting Responsibly	EM-6: Valuing Traditions and Institutions
	EM-7: Developing Ethical Identity and Integrity

*Implementing the ethical action by knowing how to do so
and following through despite hardship.*

Once Mr. Anderson has determined his priorities, he must complete the action and this requires ethical action. Ethical action involves two aspects: ego strength, the ability to persevere despite obstacles and opposition, and implementation skills, knowing what steps to take in order to complete the ethical action.

Ethical Action

Judge the feasibility of the chosen option
What is my attitude about taking this action? Do I believe it is possible for me to take this action? Do I believe that it is likely I will succeed?

Take action
What steps need to be taken to complete the action? Whose help do I need in my family/community/affiliative group? What back up plan do I have if this doesn't work?

Follow through
How do I help myself follow through on this action? How can others help me follow through? How do I resist giving up? How do I muster the courage to do it?

Reflect
What were the consequences of my decision? How did the decision affect me/my family/community/affiliative groups? Did the results turn out as I planned? In the future, should I change the decision or the decision process?

In our situation, Mr. Anderson might be very tired and have to draw up his strength and energize himself in order to take action. The implementation skills required in our scenario might include the manner of Mr. Anderson's intervention (e.g., severe and degrading reprimand versus a kind but firm reproach; or a culturally-sensitive approach that saves a student's 'face').

Let us consider another example. Perhaps a teacher knows that one of her students is smoking when he goes to the lavatory and she believes that it is best to stop him. Ethical action means that she has the action or fortitude to complete the ethical course of action. Many obstacles can arise to circumvent taking the ethical action. For example, if the student is 6 1/2 feet tall, she may feel physically threatened by the thought of confronting him and not even try. On the other hand, she may or may not know what steps to take to handle the situation. For example, to overcome fear for personal safety, she could ask another (bigger) teacher to help her or may inform the head of the school.

ETHICAL ACTION SKILLS
EA-1: Resolving Conflicts and Problems
EA-2: Asserting Respectfully
EA-3: Taking Initiative as a Leader
EA-4: Planning to Implement Decisions
EA-5: Cultivating Courage
EA-6: Persevering
EA-7: Working Hard

Need for All the Processes

These processes—ethical sensitivity, ethical judgment, ethical motivation, and ethical action—comprise the minimal amount of psychological processing that must occur for an ethical behavior to result. They are highly interdependent. That is, all the processes must be successfully completed before ethical behavior takes place. If one process fails, ethical action will not occur. For instance, if a teacher is highly sensitive to her students and environment but makes poor decisions (e.g., bargaining with students for their cooperation each day), poor outcomes may result. Or, a teacher may be sensitive to the situation, make a responsible ethical judgment, be highly motivated, but lack the backbone to follow through when a student challenges his action.

The processes also interact. That is, one may be so focused on one of the processes that it affects another process. For instance, the teacher who fears for her own safety or who values peace within the classroom may not challenge the students but try to keep them happy by not confronting any miscreant behaviors. Or, a teacher who is extremely tired and wanting to go home to rest may also be less sensitive to the needs of his students and miss cues that indicate ethical conflict.

Teaching Students Ethical Skills

The four-process model outlined here is helpful when thinking about designing instruction to promote ethical behavior. Like teachers, students face ethical dilemmas and situations each day. They have countless opportunities to demonstrate civic and ethical behavior. Their responses may be thoughtful and considerate or may be thoughtless and harmful to self and others. The teacher has a unique opportunity to help students nurture thoughtfulness and consideration of others. Our framework is intended to provide goals for teachers to do so. Our guide booklets suggest methods for reaching these goals during regular instruction.

We parcel each of the four processes into skills. The categorization of skills is not exhaustive but consists of skills that can be taught in a public school classroom. (There are other aspects of the processes that are either controversial or difficult to implement and assess in the public school classroom.) On the next page, we list the whole set of skills that are discussed in the guide booklets.

Ethical Behavior Skills for the Ethical Process Model

Activity Booklet 1: ETHICAL SENSITIVITY
ES-1: Understanding Emotional Expression
ES-2: Taking the Perspective of Others
ES-3: Connecting to Others
ES-4: Responding to Diversity
ES-5: Controlling Social Bias
ES-6: Interpreting Situations
ES-7: Communicating Well

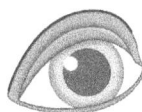

Activity Booklet 2: ETHICAL JUDGMENT
EJ-1: Reasoning Generally
EJ-2: Reasoning Ethically
EJ-3: Understanding Ethical Problems
EJ-4: Using Codes and Identifying Judgment Criteria
EJ-5: Understanding Consequences
EJ-6: Reflecting on the Process and Outcome
EJ-7: Coping

Activity Booklet 3: ETHICAL MOTIVATION
EM-1: Respecting Others
EM-2: Cultivating Conscience
EM-3: Acting Responsibly
EM-4: Being a Community Member
EM-5: Finding Meaning in Life
EM-6: Valuing Traditions and Institutions
EM-7: Developing Ethical Identity and Integrity

Activity Booklet 4: ETHICAL ACTION
EA-1: Resolving Conflicts and Problems
EA-2: Asserting Respectfully
EA-3: Taking Initiative as a Leader
EA-4: Planning to Implement Decisions
EA-5: Cultivating Courage
EA-6: Persevering
EA-7: Working Hard

How Should Character Be Taught?
Development Through Levels of Expertise

Each process of the Ethical Expertise Model is divided into several skills. The skills in each process include elements that we think are fundamental and have aspects that can be taught.

We present the skills in terms of expertise development. Think about how a young child learns to talk. First the child is exposed to sounds of all sorts, rather quickly learning the specialness of speech sounds in the environment. The child begins to make sounds, later to mimic and have mock conversations with a responsive caregiver. After many months, an actual word is spoken. From there, the child adds to his or her vocabulary little by little and then in floods. Think of how many hours a child has heard speech before age 2. Think of how much there is to learn yet after age 2. There are many phases of development in language acquisition and mastery. These phases (or levels) are movements toward expertise—toward the eloquence of an Eleanor Roosevelt or William F. Buckley, Jr. We use the notion of expertise in making recommendations for instruction.

Why Use an Expertise Approach?

Billy has an IQ of 121 on a standardized individual intelligence test; Jimmy has an IQ of 94 on the same test. What do each of these scores, and the difference between them, mean? The ... best available answer to this question is quite different from the one that is conventionally offered—that the scores and the difference between them reflect not some largely inborn, relatively fixed ability construct, but rather a construct of developing expertise. I refer to the expertise that all of these assessments measure as developing rather than as developed because expertise is typically not at an end state but is in a process of continual development. (Sternberg, 1998, p. 11)

Current understanding of knowledge acquisition adopts the construct of novice-to-expert learning. According to this paradigm, individuals build their knowledge over time during the course of experience related to the knowledge domain. Robert Sternberg is a world-renown expert on human abilities and cognition who contends that abilities are developing expertise. Standardized tests measure how much expertise you've developed in a particular subject area or domain (and how much expertise you have at taking such tests).

In general, what do experts have that novices do not have?
Here is a list that Sternberg (1998) garners from research.
- Experts have large, rich, organized networks of concepts (schemas) containing a great deal of declarative knowledge about the domain
- Experts have well-organized, higher interconnected units of knowledge in the domain

What can experts do that novices cannot do?
Sternberg (1998) says that experts can:

- Develop sophisticated representations of domain problems based on structural similarities
- Work forward from given information to implement strategies for finding unknowns in problem solving
- Choose a strategy based on elaborate schemas for problem solving
- Use automated sequences of steps in problem solving
- Demonstrate highly efficient problem solving
- Accurately predict the difficulty of solving certain problems
- Carefully monitor their own problem-solving strategies and process
- Demonstrate high accuracy in reaching appropriate solutions to problems

The level of expertise described by Sternberg requires extensive study and deliberate practice. In primary and secondary schooling, there are many subjects to be covered and little time to spend on each one. Nevertheless, teachers can approach the subject matter as a domain of knowledge that novices can, over time, learn to master. Nurturing mastery of a domain is a lifelong endeavor. Teachers have a chance to help students develop the attitudes and motivation to monitor their own progress toward expertise.

How can novices develop expertise?
Sternberg (1998) suggests that novices should:

- Receive direct instruction to build a knowledge base (lecture, tutoring)
- Engage in actual problem solving
- Engage in role modeling of expert behavior
- Think about problems in the domain and how to solve them
- Receive rewards for successful solution of domain problems

For each skill in a process, we have condensed the complex acquisition of expertise into five skill levels (a larger number would be unmanageable). The purpose of the levels is to give teachers an idea of what students need for developing the given skill, knowledge, or attitude, or what kinds of behavior exhibit a certain level of expertise development. The levels refer to phases of development as both a process (ways to learn a skill) and a product (skills learned). Within each level are many sublevels and supplementary skills that we have not attempted to name. Instead, we use terms that point to the broad processes of building expertise in the domain. The levels are cumulative, that is, each level builds on the previous level. Further, within each skill are many domains. To develop new skills in a domain, the individual circles back through the levels to develop expertise.

Novice-expert differences in the skill categories
Some skill categories are learned from infancy for most people, requiring little conscious effort. For example, *Reading and Expressing Emotion* comes about naturally as a part of learning to get along with others. However, not everyone learns these skills, or learns them well, and few learn them across cultural contexts. Therefore, we include these 'naturally-acquired' skills as areas for all to expand cross-culturally and for some to learn explicitly.

Other skill categories are not learned as a matter of course during childhood. Instead they require concentrated effort. For example, *Controlling Social Bias* does not come naturally to any human or human group. We include these 'studied' skills because they are critical for ethical behavior.

Breaking down the skill category
Although we have parsed the processes into skill categories, the skill categories themselves can be broken down further into sub-skills. <u>We encourage you and your team to do this as much as possible.</u> When you do this, consider what a novice (someone who knows nothing or very little) would need to learn.

On the next page is a brief description of each level of expertise.

Levels of Expertise of an Ethical Behavior Skill

LEVEL 1: IMMERSION IN EXAMPLES AND OPPORTUNITIES
Attend to the big picture, Learn to recognize basic patterns

The teacher plunges students into multiple, engaging activities. Students learn to recognize broad patterns in the domain (identification knowledge). They develop gradual awareness and recognition of elements in the domain.

LEVEL 2: ATTENTION TO FACTS AND SKILLS
Focus on detail and prototypical examples, Build knowledge

The teacher focuses the student's attention on the elemental concepts in the domain in order to build elaboration knowledge. Skills are gradually acquired through motivated, focused attention.

LEVEL 3: PRACTICE PROCEDURES
Set goals, Plan steps of problem solving, Practice skills

The teacher coaches the student and allows the student to try out many skills and ideas throughout the domain to build an understanding of how these relate and how best to solve problems in the domain (planning knowledge). Skills are developed through practice and exploration

LEVEL 4: INTEGRATE KNOWLEDGE AND PROCEDURES
Execute plans, Solve problems

The student finds numerous mentors and/or seeks out information to continue building concepts and skills. There is a gradual systematic integration and application of skills across many situations. The student learns how to take the steps in solving complex domain problems (execution knowledge).

Who Decides Which Values to Teach?
The community

We have presented a set of ethical skills selected according to what enables a person to get along ethically with others and to thrive as a human being. The skills are to be taught developmentally, helping students build expertise. But what do the ethical skills actually look like? For example, what does "respecting others" look like? If one were to travel around the world, the answer would vary. While respect itself is a value worldwide, each community has its own understanding of how it should look. For example, to show respect in some cultures, one speaks quietly and demurely with little eye contact. In other cultures, respect involves looking others in the eye and expressing one's opinions openly. Likewise, "communicating well" or "identifying consequences" can vary across communities. In other words, while in its essence an ethical skill is the same across contexts, it may look different. In the EthEx Model, students learn the different ways a skill appears in their community.

The EthEx Model project emphasizes the importance of embedding the skill categories in community cultural contexts. We encourage communities to be involved in the specific aspects of creating a curriculum for skill development. We hope that the actual day-to-day practice of the skills be determined on site, in the community. Students can gather information about the skill from the community (parents, elders) and bring back that information to the classroom. The teacher can tailor the classroom work to the local understanding of the skill. If there are many interpretations of the skills because of diverse families, this diversity is brought into the classroom by the students themselves.

The goal of any character education program is to build good community members, for it is in communities that students express their values, make ethical decisions, and take ethical action. To be an effective community member in the United States, students need skills for democratic citizenship. These skills are included in the list of ethical skills.

What Is the Student's Role?
To decide his or her own character

The student is not a passive trainee in an EthEx classroom. Through classroom posters and bookmarks, each student is encouraged to think about the following questions: "Who should I be? What should I become?" As teachers approach each skill, these are the questions that should be raised. The teacher can ask students about each skill category, "How do you want to be known?— as [a good communicator, a problem solver, a leader]?" Sometimes the teacher has to identify a particular adult that the student trusts and ask, "What would [so and so] want you to be?" Every day, students should feel empowered with the knowledge that they are creating their own characters with the decisions they make and the actions they take.

The EthEx Model includes both **skills for personal development** and **skills for getting along with others**. All skills are necessary for ethical personhood. The better one knows oneself, the better one can control and guide the self, and the better able one can interact respectfully with others. On the next page we list the skills and the primary focus of each one, which is either on the self or others.

Ethical Behavior Categories for Each Process

The categories are skills the individual needs to develop for reaching individual potential and skills for living a cooperative life with others.

Process Skills	Focus
ETHICAL SENSITIVITY	
ES-1: Understanding Emotional Expression	Self and Others
ES-2: Taking the Perspective of Others	Others
ES-3: Connecting to Others	Others
ES-4: Responding to Diversity	Self and Others
ES-5: Controlling Social Bias	Self
ES-6: Interpreting Situations	Self and Others
ES-7: Communicating Well	Self and Others
ETHICAL JUDGMENT	
EJ-1: Reasoning Generally	Self
EJ-2: Reasoning Ethically	Self
EJ-3: Understanding Ethical Problems	Self and Others
EJ-4: Using Codes and Identifying Judgment Criteria	Self
EJ-5: Understanding Consequences	Self and Others
EJ-6: Reflecting on the Process and Outcome	Self and Others
EJ-7: Coping	Self
ETHICAL MOTIVATION	
EM-1: Respecting Others	Others
EM-2: Cultivating Conscience	Self
EM-3: Acting Responsibly	Self and Others
EM-4: Being a Community Member	Others
EM-5: Finding Meaning in Life	Self and Others
EM-6: Valuing Traditions and Institutions	Self and Others
EM-7: Developing Ethical Identity and Integrity	Self
ETHICAL ACTION	
EA-1: Resolving Conflicts and Problems	Self and Others
EA-2: Asserting Respectfully	Self and Others
EA-3: Taking Initiative as a Leader	Self and Others
EA-4: Planning to Implement Decisions	Self and Others
EA-5: Cultivating Courage	Self and Others
EA-6: Persevering	Self and Others
EA-7: Working Hard	Self

When Should Character Be Taught?
During regular instruction

EthEx stresses the importance of embedding character education into regular, academic, and standards-based instruction. We believe that character education should not stand alone but be incorporated into the entire spectrum of education for students. Regardless of the curriculum, teachers can always raise issues of ethics in lessons.

The second section of this book offers suggestions on how to integrate character development into regular academic instruction. The suggestions in this book are for only one of four processes. We hope you pick up the other three books in order to promote skill development in all processes and skills.

Characteristics of the EthEx Model

Provides a concrete view of ethical behavior
described in *What Should Be Taught?* section (pp. 9-19)

Focuses on novice-to-expert skill building
described in *How Should Character Be Taught?* section (pp. 20-23)

Addresses community cultural contexts
described in *Who Decides Which Values to Teach?* section (p. 24)

Empowers the student
described in *What Is the Student's Role?* section (pp. 25-26)

Embeds character education into regular instruction
described in *When Should Character Be Taught?* section (p. 27)

Ethical Sensitivity
How Ethical Sensitivity Skills Fit with Virtues

VIRTUE \ SUBSKILL	ES-1 Emotional Expression	ES-2 Taking Persectives	ES-3 Connecting to Others	ES-4 Diversity	ES-5 Controlling Social Bias	ES-6 Interpret Situations	ES-7 Communic-ating Well
Altruism		*	*			*	
Citizenship		*			*	*	*
Civility			*				*
Commitment			*				
Compassion	*	*	*				
Cooperation			*	*	*		*
Courage							
Courtesy			*	*	*		*
Duty							
Fairness		*			*		
Faith			*				
Forbearance	*	*			*		
Foresight		*				*	
Forgiveness					*		
Friendship			*	*			*
Generosity		*	*				
Graciousness	*		*	*		*	*
Hard work							
Helpfulness		*	*			*	
Honesty	*		*				*
Honor							
Hopefulness						*	
Includes others		*	*	*	*	*	*
Justice		*			*		
Kindness	*		*				*
Lawfulness							
Loyalty			*	*			
Obedience							
Obligation							
Patience	*					*	*
Patriotism					*		
Persistence							
Personal Responsibility		*				*	
Politeness	*		*				A
Respect	*		*		*		*
Reverence			*				
Self-control	*						*
Self-sacrifice							
Social Responsibility		*		*	*	*	
Tolerance	*	*		*	*		
Trustworthiness			*				
Unselfishness		*					

Ethical Judgment
How Ethical Judgment Skills Fit with Virtues

VIRTUE \ SUBSKILL	EJ-1 Reasoning Generally	EJ-2 Reasoning Ethically	EJ-3 Understand Problems	EJ-4 Using Codes	EJ-5 Conse-quences	EJ-6 Reflecting	EJ-7 Coping
Altruism		*		*		*	
Citizenship		*	*	*		*	
Civility		*		*		*	
Commitment		*		*	*	*	*
Compassion		*	*	*		*	
Cooperation		*				*	
Courage							
Courtesy		*		*		*	
Duty		*		*		*	
Faith		*		*		*	*
Fairness		*	*	*		*	
Forgiveness				*		*	
Friendship		*		*			
Forbearance		*		*		*	*
Foresight	*	*		*			
Generosity		*		*		*	
Graciousness				*			*
Hard work	*	*					
Helpfulness		*		*		*	
Honor		*		*		*	
Honesty		*		*		*	
Hopefulness							*
Includes others		*		*		*	
Justice		*	*	*		*	
Kindness		*		*		*	
Lawfulness		*	*	*		*	
Loyalty		*		*		*	
Obedience		*		*		*	
Obligation		*	*	*		*	
Patience	*				*		*
Patriotism		*		*		*	
Persistence	*						
Politeness				*			
Respect		*		*		*	*
Reverence		*		*		*	*
Personal Responsibility	*	*	*	*		*	
Social Responsibility		*	*	*	*	*	
Self-control					*		*
Self-sacrifice		*				*	
Tolerance		*		*		*	*
Trustworthiness							*
Unselfishness		*		*		*	

Ethical Motivation
How Ethical Motivation Skills Fit with Virtues

SUBSKILL / VIRTUE	EM-1 Respecting Others	EM-2 Cultivating Conscience	EM-3 Acting Responsibly	EM-4 Community Member	EM-5 Finding Meaning	EM-6 Valuing Traditions	EM-7 Ethical Identity
Altruism				*	*		*
Citizenship	*	*	*	*		*	
Civility	*	*					*
Commitment		*	*	*	*	*	*
Compassion	*			*	*		*
Cooperation	*	*	*	*	*	*	
Courage		*		*	*		*
Courtesy	*						
Duty	*	*	*			*	
Faith				*	*		*
Fairness				*		*	
Forgiveness	*				*		
Friendship	*						
Forbearance	*	*		*			
Foresight	*		*		*	*	*
Generosity				*			*
Graciousness	*			*			
Hard work			*	*		*	*
Helpfulness	*		*	*			
Honor		*	*		*	*	*
Honesty	*	*					
Hopefulness	*		*	*	*	*	*
Includes others	*			*		*	
Justice						*	
Kindness	*			*			*
Lawfulness		*	*			*	*
Loyalty		*	*			*	*
Obedience		*					
Obligation		*	*	*			
Patience	*		*	*	*	*	
Patriotism						*	
Persistence			*		*	*	*
Politeness	*			*			
Respect	*	*	*	*	*	*	*
Reverence	*	*	*	*	*	*	
Personal Responsibility	*	*	*			*	*
Social Responsibility	*		*	*		*	*
Self-control	*	*	*	*	*		*
Self-sacrifice		*		*			*
Tolerance	*	*	*	*		*	
Trustworthiness		*		*			*
Unselfishness	*	*	*	*	*		*

Ethical Action
How Ethical Action Skills Fit with Virtues

VIRTUE · SUBSKILL	EA-1 Resolving Conflicts	EA-2 Assertive-ness	EA-3 Initiative as Leader	EA-4 Planning	EA-5 Cultivating Courage	EA-6 Persevering	EA-7 Working Hard
Altruism			*		*	*	
Citizenship	*		*	*	*	*	*
Civility	*	*				*	
Commitment	*	*	*	*	*	*	*
Compassion		*	*	*	*		*
Cooperation	*	*	*	*			*
Courage		*	*		*		
Courtesy	*	*					
Duty	*		*	*	*	*	*
Fairness	*				*		
Faith			*	*	*		*
Forbearance	*	*	*		*	*	*
Foresight	*	*	*				*
Forgiveness							
Friendship	*			*			
Generosity			*		*		
Graciousness							
Hard work		*	*	*	*	*	*
Helpfulness			*		*	*	*
Honesty		*	*	*			
Honor	*		*	*	*		*
Hopefulness	*	*	*				
Includes others	*		*	*			
Justice	*			*	*		*
Kindness							
Lawfulness			*	*			*
Loyalty			*	*			*
Obedience							*
Obligation	*		*	*			*
Patience	*	*	*			*	*
Patriotism			*	*	*		
Persistence	*	*	*		*	*	*
Personal Responsibility	*		*		*	*	*
Politeness		*		*			
Respect	*	*	*	*			
Reverence			*	*			
Self-control	*	*	*	*		*	*
Self-sacrifice			*		*	*	
Social Responsibility	*		*		*	*	*
Tolerance	*	*	*				
Trustworthiness		*	*				
Unselfishness	*		*	*	*		

References

Bebeau, M., Rest, J. R., & Narvaez, D. (1999). Beyond the promise: A framework for research in moral education. *Educational Researcher, 28*(4), 18-26.

Bellah, R., Madsen, R., Sullivan, W., Swidler, A., & Tipton, S. (1985). *Habits of the heart: Individualism and commitment in American life.* Berkeley: University of California Press.

Bergem, T. (1990). The teacher as moral agent. *Journal of Ethical Education, 19*(2), 88-100.

Blasi, A. (1984). Moral identity: Its role in moral functioning. In W. M. Kurtines & J. L. Gewirtz (Eds.), *Morality, moral behavior, and moral development* (pp. 128-139). New York: Wiley-Interscience.

Damon, W. (1984). Self-understanding and moral development from childhood to adolescence. In W. M. Kurtines & J. L. Gewirtz (Eds.), *Morality, moral behavior, and moral development* (pp. 109-127). New York: Wiley-Interscience.

Etzioni, A. (1994). *The spirit of community: The reinvention of American society.* New York: Simon & Schuster.

Faul, S. (1994). *Xenophobe's guide to the Americans.* London: Ravette.

Goodlad, J., Soder, R., & Sirotnik, K. (1990). *The moral dimensions of teaching.* San Francisco: Jossey-Bass.

Kohlberg, L. (1984). *The psychology of moral development.* New York: Harper & Row.

National Education Association. (1975). *Code of ethics of the education profession.* Retrieved February 5, 2009, from http://ethics.iit.edu/codes/coe/nat.edu.assoc.1975.html

Rest, J. R. (1979). *Development in judging moral issues.* Minneapolis: University of Minnesota Press.

Rest, J. R. (1983). Morality. In P. Mussen (Series Ed.), J. Flavell & E. Markham, (Volume Eds.), *Manual of child psychology: Vol. 3, Cognitive development* (pp. 556-269). New York: Wiley.

Rest, J. R. (1986). *Moral development: Advances in research and theory.* New York: Praeger.

Steinberg, L. (1996). *Beyond the classroom: Why school reform failed and what parents need to do.* New York: Simon and Schuster.

Sternberg, R. (1998). Abilities are forms of developing expertise. *Educational Researcher, 3*, 22-35.

Nurturing Ethical Action

Organization of Ethical Action Booklet

Overview Pages
Ethical Action skills and subskills

Subskill Sections (7 skill sections in all—the "meat" of the booklet)
Skill Overview (see sample page below)
Subskills (see sample pages on p. 37)
    Activities
    Assessment hints
    Climate suggestions

Appendix
Guide for Lesson Planning
'Linking to the Community' Worksheet
Rubric Examples
Special Activities
Resources
Linking EA Skills to Search Institute Assets
References

Skill Overview Page

Skill Title

WHAT the skill is

WHY the skill is important

SUBSKILLS list

Persevering

Ethical Action 6

WHAT
Perseverance enables individuals to complete actions that are important to them and others. Without it, many ethical actions would fail at the sight of the first obstacle or difficulty.

WHY
Perseverance is important for the completion of an ethical action. Children can be successfully instructed to 'talk to themselves' about not doing something, and instructed on how to distract themselves from unwanted behavior. A form of self-talk to complete a task can be a useful technique to help one find the ego strength to complete an ethical action—at any age.

EA-6 Developing Perseverance: Overview

SUBSKILLS OVERVIEW
Be steadfast
Overcome obstacles
Build competence

Skill Name: Subskill Name
Side Header

Ethical Action Overview

Subskill Activities Page

Skill & Subskill NAME

Expert Example

Subskill Activities by Level of Expertise
(4 levels total, usually spans 2-4 pages per subskill)

Persevering by Building Competence

Expert

Christopher Reeves (who played Superman in the movies) had an equestrian accident that left him a quadriplegic. He could have given up in life and stayed home quietly, but he became a spokesman for those with spinal injuries, traveling to speak about the importance of research in spinal injuries.

Ideas for Developing Skills

Level 1: Immersion in Examples and Opportunities
Attend to the big picture, Learn to recognize basic patterns

Study self-efficacy. Discuss how, for a particular field, small successes give a person confidence to keep trying and try harder things. Find examples in literature, television and movies, or in a particular subject area. ★

Level 2: Attention to Facts and Skills
Focus on detail and prototypical examples, Build knowledge

Self-talk. Find examples of and discuss how to 'cheerlead' for yourself in different situations. What behaviors help you do your best and reach excellence? (1) Students discuss self-talk and behaviors that help one persevere. (2) Students interview older students or adults about general behaviors. (3) Students interview adults in roles they admire or strive for in a particular field. ★

Level 3: Practice Procedures
Set goals, Plan steps of problem solving, Practice skills

Examples of pushing oneself in helping others. Students interview elders about their personal experiences of (1) how they persevered in trying to help others; (2) how they persevered in working towards a goal that helped humanity.

Level 4: Integrate Knowledge and Procedures
Execute Plans, Solve Problems

Self-help. Have students practice ways to coach oneself to reach excellence in ... in mental and physical ... eting tasks without

EA-6 Developing Perseverance: Building competence

Assessment Hints

Building Competence

Use multiple-choice, true-false, short answer, or essay tests to assess student's knowledge of strategies to push oneself.

Have students write reports, based on observations or interviews, of what they learned about pushing oneself.

**Skill Name:
Subskill Name**
Side Header

Hints for Assessment

Skill Climate Page

Create a Climate to Persevere

Regularly discuss the importance of finishing a task, as a group or individual.

Regularly point out what would happen if people did not persevere until a job was done (e.g., the highway, a bridge, your house, your car) and how it would affect people around them.

Discuss the importance of persevering in meeting your responsibilities to others.

Sample Student Self Monitoring
Persevering

Be steadfast
I wait to reward myself until I've finished my work.
I don't wait until the last minute to do my work.
I lose control when I am angry. (NOT)
I control my feelings of anger.
I resist my impulses to disobey rules.

What you need to know for success in school

1. That attitudes affect behavior
2. That what you believe/think about affects your behavior
3. That you have some control over your attitudes
4. That learning anything requires commitment (decision to put your energies into a task)

EA-6 Developing Perseverance: Climate

Suggestions for Creating a Climate to Develop Skill

Sample Self-Monitoring Questions for Student

Selections to Post in the Classroom for Developing Skill

Ethical Action Overview

Ethical Processes & Skills
with Ethical Action Subskills

Activity Booklet 1: ETHICAL SENSITIVITY
ES-1 Understanding Emotional Expression
ES-2 Taking the Perspective of Others
ES-3 Connecting to Others
ES-4 Responding to Diversity
ES-5 Controlling Social Bias
ES-6 Interpreting Situations
ES-7 Communicating Well

Activity Booklet 2: ETHICAL JUDGMENT
EJ-1 Reasoning Generally
EJ-2 Reasoning Ethically
EJ-3 Understanding Ethical Problems
EJ-4 Using Codes and Identifying Judgment
     Criteria
EJ-5 Understanding Consequences
EJ-6 Reflecting on the Process and Outcome
EJ-7 Coping

Activity Booklet 3: ETHICAL MOTIVATION
EM-1 Respecting Others
EM-2 Cultivating Conscience
EM-3 Acting Responsibly
EM-4 Being a Community Member
EM-5 Finding Meaning in Life
EM-6 Valuing Traditions and Institutions
EM-7 Developing Ethical Identity and Integrity

Activity Booklet 4: ETHICAL ACTION

EA-1 Resolving Conflicts and Problems
Solve interpersonal problems
Negotiate
Make amends

EA-2 Asserting Respectfully
Attend to human needs
Build assertiveness skills
Use rhetoric respectfully

EA-3 Taking Initiative as a Leader
Be a leader
Take initiative for and with others
Mentor others

EA-4 Planning to Implement Decisions
Think strategically
Implement successfully
Determine resource use

EA-5 Cultivating Courage
Manage fear
Stand up under pressure
Manage change and uncertainty

EA-6 Persevering
Be steadfast
Overcome obstacles
Build competence

EA-7 Working Hard
Set reachable goals
Manage time
Take charge of your life

Ethical Action

Ethical Action involves implementing the ethical action by knowing how to do so
and following through despite obstacles and difficulties.

Outline of Skills

EA-1: RESOLVING CONFLICTS AND PROBLEMS

Conflicts between human beings are inevitable because we often feel different things or desire the same things. Conflicts can be approached in several ways, (a) fighting until one side gives up, (b) coercion by the side with more power, (c) ignoring as long as nothing brings the conflict into the forefront, (d) negotiation and (e) compromise. In order to truly resolve conflicts and not keep them smoldering, for example with retaliations and passive aggression, people need skills for communicating about their needs and negotiating a peaceful settlement. Another skill required for living respectfully with others is making amends.

EA-2: ASSERTING RESPECTFULLY

Assertive behavior is exerting oneself to achieve a desired goal through constructive interaction with others. On a continuum, assertiveness lies between passiveness (doing for others at the expense of achieving one's own goals) and aggressiveness (achieving one's goals at the expense of others). Assertiveness skills should be used to speak up for the needs of others. When you speak up for someone's needs, you want to persuade your audience. Persuasion skills must be used carefully so as to respect the rights and responsibilities of the listener.

EA-3: TAKING INITIATIVE AS A LEADER

Ethical character is manifested in good leaders as well as followers. An ethical leader will encourage or inspire others to follow their ethical instincts by encouraging these attitudes, knowledge and skills. Ethical leaders will modulate their form of leadership depending on the task at hand. They will also use the resources of the group to the greatest effect. Good leaders are able to mentor others in ethical leadership.

EA-4: PLANNING TO IMPLEMENT DECISIONS

Planning is a crucial step between making a judgment and carrying it out. In planning to implement an ethical decision, the student needs to think about what actions are required, possible obstacles, alternative actions, and resources that may be needed. Students need extensive practice in following through so that they can finely hone these skills and apply them in diverse situations.

EA-5: CULTIVATING COURAGE

Courage is using one's ethical integrity to stand-up for what you believe. Activities within and outside of the classroom are needed to (1) develop a sense of competence or self-efficacy, and to (2) reinforce the good feelings that can accompany taking risks for others.

EA-6: PERSEVERING

Perseverance enables individuals to complete actions that are important to them and others. Without it, many ethical actions would fail at the sight of the first obstacle or difficulty. Perseverance involves skills of steadfastness, resourcefulness and other competencies related to successful completion of goals.

EA-7: WORKING HARD

Hard work means spending a great deal of energy, time and sweat to accomplish a worthwhile task. It means continuing toward a goal even when the goal is far off and the journey gets boring or tedious. In order to work hard successfully, one must have skills of setting reachable goals, managing time and taking charge of one's life.

Ethical Action

WHAT

Ethical Action skills and attitudes lead to success in completing an ethical goal. Ethical Action includes (1) *interpersonal skills* such as conflict resolution and negotiation, leadership, assertiveness, and basic communication and (2) *personal skills* such as taking initiative, courage, perseverance, and working hard.

WHY

A person without all or most of these skills may have a difficult time accomplishing an ethical action, no matter how much he or she might feel motivated to do so. These skills make it possible to follow through and complete the identified ethical action.

ROLE OF TEACHER/ADULT

Adults help students develop ethical action skills by modeling follow-through skills, by describing ethical actions they have taken and the challenges they encountered, and by providing many opportunities for students to practice the skills.

TACKLING EXCUSES AND HANGUPS

Sometimes students will resist learning or taking action, giving excuses like the following. We offer suggestions about how to counteract these attitudes.

'Why should I bother about them?' (sense of superiority)
Discuss this as a general human bias that one must consciously control.

'Yup, I was right about those homeless people. They're just lazy.'
Discuss the human tendency to look only for confirming evidence of personal bias. Work on perspective-taking.

'I couldn't help it. I was so mad.'
Discuss or demonstrate the benefits of giving emotions a "cooling down period" and being objective.

'It's not my problem.'
Discuss human relatedness (ES-3) and ethical responsibility (EM-4).

'That looks/tastes/smells weird!'
Work on reducing fear of the unknown and difference. Discuss the realistic risks and benefits of learning about something new.

'It's just a TV show. I know it's not real.'
Discuss the harm of desensitization to violence and objectification of people.

'The consequences are too far in the future to concern me.' (This is especially pertinent to young people's attitudes toward drugs, alcohol.) Bring in guest speakers who had these thoughts/attitudes and then experienced the "far off" consequences. Encourage students to discuss issues with the speaker.

'The possible consequences will never happen to me.' (e.g., getting pregnant, being arrested for vandalism, other crimes) Bring in guest speakers who had these thoughts/attitudes and then experienced the "unrealistic" consequences. Encourage students to discuss issues with the speaker.

'The possible consequences will never happen to him/her/them.'
Bring in guest speakers who had these thoughts/attitudes and then witnessed the "improbable" consequences occurring to another (e.g., killing a friend or stranger by driving drunk). Encourage students to discuss issues with the speaker and ask many questions.

'I have no choice—my friends are making me do this.'
Have students practice assertiveness skills: (1) Describe the situation that is upsetting, without blaming or getting emotional. (2) Tell other person your feelings. (3) Tell other person what you want him/her to change. (4) Tell other person how the change would make you feel.

'It's not my fault—person X is who you should blame!'
Counter with techniques to foster feelings of responsibility/accountability for one's own actions: (1) Discipline with immediate consequences and a given reason. (2) Help parents with discipline plans that include giving reasons to students when disciplined. (3) Discuss related dilemmas with slight variations.

'I can't change this situation so I won't try.'
Counter with inspirational examples of how others make a difference (e.g., Rosa Parks, or a local community member who has made a difference). Discuss how student is more similar than different to this person. Emphasize how the student can make a difference.

Ethical Action Overview

TACKLING EXCUSES AND HANGUPS (continued)

'This situation is none of my concern.' (e.g., witnessing a fight or a crime)
Counter with citizenship activities, discussing the importance of concern for others in the community and outside of the community. Discuss the purpose of citizenship and its related responsibilities. Study exemplars of good citizenship.

'There's no time to think of other alternatives!'
Discuss (1) human tendencies to lose control (and do harm) when emotions are high, and (2) the importance of carefully and systematically thinking through a dilemma or problem and decision so others and yourself will not be harmed in the immediate or distant future.

'Why should their well-being be my concern?' (lack of positive regard for life)
Encourage a more positive regard for life and discuss in class people who have a healthy regard for life.

'It's not my responsibility to save the world!' (not seeing the value of human existence)
Counter with a discussion of the interconnectedness of us all and our ethical obligations to each other.

'Why should I help them? Nobody's ever done anything for me!' (pessimistic attitude resulting from negative life experience) Discuss the importance of optimism, and of overcoming obstacles.

'It's their own fault that they're in this mess...not mine.' (lack of empathic understanding of others) Foster a discussion of those who are empathic and how to help another in distress.

'I've got other things planned...I don't have time to help!' (having immediate needs that are in opposition to caring for others) Discuss the importance of weighing others' needs against our own, developing courtesy, meeting obligations and showing generosity.

'Being a citizen of the U.S.A. means freedom to do what I want.'
Counter with examination and discussion of various forms of citizenship. Discuss the purpose of citizenship and its related responsibilities.

'This is stuff that adults do.'
Discuss examples of the positive and meaningful impact of young people on the world (e.g., dot-com companies, altruistic group leadership, etc.).

'This is the stuff that people in x-group do.'
Give counter examples to sex-typing, group typing.

'Other people will take care of it.'
Discuss this as a general human bias.

'I don't want to look like a fool in front of my classmates.'
Discuss counter examples of young people being seen as assertive, taking action for others and standing out.

'I'm afraid that my classmates might get back at me.' (This may come up especially if the peers are involved in unethical or illegal activities.) Discuss choices of peers, role models and the consequences.

'I don't like people in that group.'
Discuss the changing nature of group membership and feeling 'outside.'

'I can't do it.'
Discuss this as an obstacle to overcome.

Ethical Action
How Ethical Action Skills Fit with Virtues

VIRTUE \ SUBSKILL	EA-1 Resolving Conflicts	EA-2 Assertive-ness	EA-3 Initiative as Leader	EA-4 Planning	EA-5 Cultivating Courage	EA-6 Persevering	EA-7 Working Hard
Altruism			*		*	*	
Citizenship	*		*	*	*	*	*
Civility	*	*				*	
Commitment	*	*	*	*	*	*	*
Compassion		*	*	*	*		*
Cooperation	*	*	*	*			*
Courage		*	*		*		
Courtesy	*	*					
Duty	*		*	*	*	*	*
Fairness	*				*		
Faith			*	*	*		*
Forbearance	*	*	*		*	*	*
Foresight	*	*	*				*
Forgiveness							
Friendship	*			*			
Generosity			*		*		
Graciousness							
Hard work		*	*	*	*	*	*
Helpfulness			*		*	*	*
Honesty		*	*	*			
Honor	*		*	*	*		*
Hopefulness	*	*	*				
Includes others	*		*	*			
Justice	*			*	*		*
Kindness							
Lawfulness			*	*			*
Loyalty			*	*			*
Obedience							*
Obligation	*		*	*			*
Patience	*	*	*			*	*
Patriotism			*	*	*		
Persistence	*	*	*		*	*	*
Personal Responsibility	*		*		*	*	*
Politeness		*		*			
Respect	*	*	*	*			
Reverence			*	*			
Self-control	*	*	*			*	*
Self-sacrifice			*		*	*	
Social Responsibility	*		*		*	*	*
Tolerance	*	*	*				
Trustworthiness		*	*				
Unselfishness	*		*	*	*		

Resolving Conflicts and Problems

(Resolve Conflicts)

WHAT

Conflicts between human beings are inevitable because we often feel different things or desire the same things. Conflicts can be approached in several ways, (a) fighting until one side gives up, (b) coercion by the side with more power, (c) ignoring as long as nothing brings the conflict into the forefront, (d) negotiation and (e) compromise. In order to truly resolve conflicts and not keep them smoldering, for example with retaliations and passive aggression, people need skills for communicating about their needs and negotiating a peaceful settlement. Another skill required for living respectfully with others is making amends.

WHY

Conflict resolution and negotiation skills are necessary for successful social interaction. Life is a series of resolving conflicts with family members, friends, co-workers, neighbors, etc. Children who are successful in getting along with others are more helpful and altruistic (Eisenberg & Mussen, 1989).

SUBSKILLS OVERVIEW

Solve Interpersonal Problems
Negotiate
Make amends

Web Wise
Worldwide Alliance of Forgiveness
      http://www.forgivenessalliance.org/day/html
Lesson plans about peace, war, conflict at
      www.esrnational.org

Resolving Conflicts by Solving Interpersonal Problems

Famous actor/comedian **Bob Hope** and singer **Dolores Reade** were married for 69 years. They had four children and pursued and achieved successful careers in the entertainment business. Bob Hope and Dolores Reade were experts in interpersonal problem solving for maintaining a happy marriage for so many years throughout their busy lives.

Creative and Expert Implementer Real-Life Example

Ideas for Developing Skills

Level 1: Immersion in Examples and Opportunities
Attend to the big picture, Learn to recognize basic patterns

Types of interpersonal conflicts. Have students keep track of conflicts between people. Bring examples to class and make a large list. Categorize the situations into groups such as: sport competition, want same thing, think differently, etc. Have students then keep track of how many of each type they encounter interpersonally over the next week. Report to class.

Study interpersonal conflict. Have students watch film about an interpersonal conflict. What was the conflict about? Discuss the perspectives of each party. Assess whether or not the outcome was successful or not. Ask students to write an alternative outcome.

Level 2: Attention to Facts and Skills
Focus on detail and prototypical examples, Build knowledge

Conflict resolution techniques. Use examples of conflicts generated previously (above). Have students learn about and practice conflict resolution techniques through role play. Assess for knowledge of techniques. (Conflict resolution curricula can be ordered through CREnet. See the Resource List for ordering information.)

Peer mediation. Teach peer mediation using one of the existing programs. (Peer mediation curricula and implementation guides can be ordered through CREnet. See the Resource List for ordering information.)

Discuss conflict resolution options. Discuss with students questions like the following: (1) What are the options when you get mad in certain situations (compare healthy and unhealthy)? (2) What are the options when someone says something mean or insulting to you (try humor)? (3) What are good and bad things about fighting (make two lists)? (4) How can you channel anger positively for change? (5) How can you counteract friends' instigation of violence? (6) How can you prepare for friends and even parents who criticize a non-violent tactic?

Starred ★ activities within each subskill go together!

Resolving Conflicts by Solving Interpersonal Problems
Ideas for Developing Skills

Level 3: Practice Procedures
Set goals, Plan steps of problem solving, Practice skills

⭐ **Create role plays of conflict situations.** Students act out conflict situations (up to point of physical contact) then create alternative endings. (Put all this on videotape for later analysis.)

Practice and assess problem-solving skills in context. (1) Structured conflict resolution: The students consider a territorial conflict between a land-locked nation and a coastal nation answering the following questions: What does each party want? What does each party feel? What are each party's reasons for their desires and feelings? Do the parties understand the opposing perspectives? If not, how can they achieve that? What are different solutions that the parties could agree on to resolve the conflict? Which one do you think is best, and why? (2) Open-ended conflict resolution: Apply the steps of conflict resolution to this conflict. Name each step and apply it to this conflict. (3) Students demonstrate conflict resolution in a particular relevant domain. Give students a description of an unresolved conflict between two individuals or groups. Ask the students to go through the necessary steps of resolving a conflict, either in written format or in a role play. (4) Essay. Students write an alternative ending to a conflict encountered in history or literature.

Fight fair. Have students role play fighting fair. Use scenarios of conflict that they have faced. Fighting fair means airing a disagreement with someone in a respectful manner. It means not running away from the disagreement, suppressing your feelings, or blowing your top. Instead, it means the following: (1) Discuss the problem as soon as possible, at a time when both people can focus on it. (2) Use "I" statements to tell the other person how you feel (e.g., "I feel angry because you did not meet me at the scheduled time."). (3) Do not use generalizations. (4) Do not use putdowns. (5) Stick to the problem at hand. (6) Attack the problem not the person. (7) Don't be defensive. Listen. (8) Try to see things from the other person's perspective. (9) When feelings get too heated, take a break and return when you have cooled down. (10) Don't make assumptions about the other person's view—ask. (11) Work as a team to solve the problem. (12) Forgive, accept and affirm the other person.

Identify and articulate different viewpoints. Students identify contrary ideas in the news or in a classroom discussion. They practice articulating different sides of a controversial issue even if he/she feels strongly about it one way or the other.

Level 4: Integrate Knowledge and Procedures
Execute plans, Solve problems

⭐ **Coaching conflict resolution.** Students help other students (same age or younger) resolve conflicts (real or hypothetical). Have the participants and the rest of the class evaluate their coaching and have them evaluate their own coaching.

Assessment Hints

Solving Interpersonal Problems Activities

Use multiple-choice, true-false, short answer, or essay tests to assess student knowledge of conflict resolution techniques.

Use a new conflict (written or video clip) and have students respond in writing how they would resolve it.

Have students role play conflict scenarios and demonstrate specific problem solving skills.

Starred ⭐ activities within each subskill go together!

Resolving Conflicts by Negotiating

Jimmy Carter, former president of the United States, has a peace center in Atlanta. Because he is renown for his negotiation skills, he is invited to countries around the world to help groups in conflict settle disagreements.

Creative and Expert Implementer Real-Life Example

Ideas for Developing Skills

Level 1: Immersion in Examples and Opportunities
Attend to the big picture, Learn to recognize basic patterns

The nature of conflict. Discuss how conflict is a normal part of human life and that moral (or ethical) conflict is necessary and inevitable in life. Getting along with others has to do with negotiating 'my wants with your wants.' Have students find examples of conflict and negotiation.

Aspects of successful negotiation. (1) Invite a local mediator (or some type of negotiator) to discuss mediation/negotiation with the students. Have them describe the steps they take, pitfalls and challenges. (2) Present to students film clips or written excerpts from accounts of successful negotiation. Students identify common characteristics. **Assess** their responses to a new conflict.

Level 2: Attention to Facts and Skills
Focus on detail and prototypical examples, Build knowledge

Group decision making. Students discuss a conflict situation in small groups. Each group discusses the positive ways to handle the situation with these instructions: Develop several possible courses of action and choose among them; develop pros and cons for each possible action. Remain flexible; try another course of action if others did not work.

Negotiations in the public sector. Study historic negotiations in the public sector. For example, negotiations about environmental policies (e.g., demonstrations against the Trident submarine, against the World Trade Organization) or about negotiation during standoffs between authority figures and citizens (e.g., Ruby Ridge, Waco). How did or didn't the parties negotiate? What was each party's perspective? Was the outcome satisfactory to both sides? What could have been done differently?

Resolving Conflicts by Negotiating
Ideas for Developing Skills
Level 2 (continued)

⭐ **Basic negotiation.** With simple, everyday scenarios like the following, have students practice the steps listed below. Scenario: (a) both students want to use the same computer; (b) my brother wants to play his stereo loudly but I want to do my homework; (c) I want to watch x television show but my sister wants to watch y; (d) one student wants the window open, the other wants it closed. Basic steps: (1) Figure out and agree on what the problem or conflict is. What are your needs? What are the other person's needs? (2) State the reasons for your viewpoint and listen to the other person's reasons. (3) Show that you understand the other person's perspective by paraphrasing what they said. (4) Come up with at least 3 possible solutions that address both of your needs. (5) Agree on one of the solutions and carry it out. (6) Check back later to see if it's working and make changes if you need to.

Starred ⭐ activities within each subskill go together!

Level 3: Practice Procedures
Set goals, Plan steps of problem solving, Practice skills

⭐ **Advanced negotiation.** Johnson (1993) suggests several steps that should be taken in a negotiation. Have students practice these during role play. (1) Agree on a definition of the conflict or problem by describing what you want, how you feel, and listening to the other person's wants and feelings. After this, agree you have a mutual problem, but one that is small and specific. (2) After expressing your interest in cooperation now and in the future, state the reasons underlying your viewpoint and listen to the other person's reasons. Focus on wants and needs, not positions. (3) Understand the other person's perspective. Paraphrase what the person said to make sure you got it right. Make sure the differences are clear to each of you. (4) Empower the other person by presenting flexible options. Come up with a number of creative, win-win solutions. (5) Set up an agreement that meets the needs of both participants, that both agree is fair, that can be justified, that strengthens your ability to work together. (6) Set up a time in the future to check on whether things are going as planned. Role plays could include: (a) your brother wants the last piece of cake and so do you; (b) your mom wants you to babysit your little sister but you want to go to the park with friends; (c) you want to participate in the local recycling program but your parents don't want to take the trouble; (d) you want to go to the party with your friends but you don't want to smoke or drink like they plan to do.

Scenarios of conflict. Students find examples in which there is a conflict between individuals or groups and act them out with several alternative endings using negotiation skills.

Balancing competing interests in negotiation. The student takes on the role of a judge and negotiates a dispute between neighbors who want control of the stream that runs between their properties. Fellow students and teacher assess their success.

Assessment Hints

Negotiation Activities

Use multiple-choice, true-false, short answer, or essay tests to assess student knowledge of negotiation skills.

Use a real-life, current conflict (written or video clip) and have students respond in writing how they would negotiate to resolve it.

Have students role play conflict scenarios and demonstrate negotiation skills.

EA-1 Resolving Conflicts and Problems

Resolving Conflicts
by Negotiating
Ideas for Developing Skills

Level 3 (continued)

Negotiations among citizen groups. Study the negotiations of citizen groups locally or nationally in one or more areas (e.g., what books should be in the school library, how to develop a certain part of town, how to alleviate poverty in the community, how to zone neighborhoods). Students analyze and report on whether or not the parties used negotiation skills (from Level 2).

Study a famous negotiation. Read about a historic negotiation and analyze which steps were taken in the process. Were the results fair? Possibilities for study are: (a) Peace agreements in areas of conflict such as the Middle East (e.g., Oslo agreement); Northern Ireland; between Ethiopia and Eritrea; Falklands war between Britain and Argentina; India's independence from Britain; the end of apartheid in South Africa; (b) environmental agreements on whaling, fishing, polluted emissions; (c) trade agreements like the North American Free Trade Agreement between the U.S. and Mexico.

Level 4: Integrate Knowledge and Procedures
Execute plans, Solve problems

Coaching others on negotiation. Using the following techniques (from Level 2), apply them to an actual situation or role play: (1) separate the people from the problem; (2) focus on interests not positions; (3) generate a variety of possibilities before deciding what to do; (4) insist that the result be based on some (jointly searched) objective standard (agreed upon outcomes). Determine success according to the satisfaction of the parties at the conclusion. See Fisher, Ury, and Patton's (1991) *Getting to Yes* for a more detailed description of this process.

Use democratic procedures in the school or classroom. Set up a classroom or school structure that reflects the "Just community," a type of school in which teachers and students share responsibility for the welfare of all students and share the process of governance. Teachers and students meet weekly to set rules and decide on punishments for rule-breaking. A fairness committee of students and teachers deal with conflict resolution and discipline. During meetings and committee meetings values and morals are discussed as expectations and values underlying rules are discussed. The teachers and students support norms that nurture community bonding. All community members are expected to care for one another. The teachers help students take on as much responsibility as they are able. You might role play this if it is not possible to actually implement. Use this website to get more information: http://tigger.uic.edu/~lnucci/MoralEd/articles/powerjust.html.

Choose an issue and work to solve it using negotiation. Have students select an issue in the school or neighborhood that they feel strongly about and would like to change. It should be a problem that is negotiable. There are specific steps to use for social action listed in EA-3, Be a leader. Emphasize using negotiation as a means to solve the problem.

Starred ★ activities
within each subskill
go together!

EA-1 Resolving Conflicts and Problems

Resolving Conflicts by Making Amends

Creative and Expert
Implementer
Real-Life Example

The concept of forgiveness is an essential part of prosocial behavior. Sometimes conflict goes too far and one or more sides are deeply injured. In this situation, the skills and attitudes of forgiveness can be helpful in preventing endless retaliation and injury. It is also a friendship skill as well as a more general interpersonal competence skill. Being able to forgive can counteract holding grudges, which contributes to much of the anger and violence in our society.

Nelson Mandela and **Desmond Tutu**, both of whom suffered under the Apartheid regime in South Africa, have worked tirelessly to bring healing and forgiveness to the nation after the fall of Apartheid rule.

Ideas for Developing Skills

Level 1: Immersion in Examples and Opportunities
Attend to the big picture, Learn to recognize basic patterns

Contrasting forgiveness with grudges. Present students with different video and story scenarios, and ask students to discriminate between forgiveness and grudges. The class discusses them, distinguishing between forgiveness and grudges.

Gathering examples of forgiveness. Have students find examples of forgiveness and grudges (1) from books, or the web, (2) from family and community members. Students report on findings and (a) create posters about letting go of grudges and (b) forgiving others.

Gathering examples of repentance and apology. Have students find examples of repentance and apology: (1) from books, or the web, (2) from family and community members. Students report on findings and (a) create posters about repenting and (b) apologizing.

Restorative justice. Restorative justice is a way to solve interpersonal problems where someone has wronged another. The emphasis is on victims helping re-integrate the offender into the community. Methods to do this include mediation, acts of reparation, financial compensation, community service, confronting the offender with the pain and suffering of the victim, shaming the offender and negotiating acts of recompense. Bring in experts in restorative justice. Have them demonstrate and discuss how it works.

Peace circles. Peace circles can be used in the classroom to discuss and resolve difficult issues or conflicts. The parties in conflict express themselves before the group. The group helps in creating solutions that all parties can agree upon.

Resolving Conflicts by Making Amends
Ideas for Developing Skills

Level 2: Attention to Facts and Skills
Focus on detail and prototypical examples, Build knowledge

Forgiveness skills. First, discuss with the students the importance of forgiveness (versus harboring grudges) in terms of getting along with others, maintaining relationships, and physical health. Then discuss the importance of communicating feelings and conflict resolution skills and how the skills can be skills of forgiveness. Discussion should also include how to know if a student truly forgave another or if it was insincere.

Practicing forgiveness and avoiding grudges. Have students identify ways that others have harmed them (or use a story as a source for ideas). Have students figure out in groups how a person might respond to such a situation. Have students role play the best ideas.

Learning from elders about forgiveness. Students interview elders about a situation in which the elder forgave another for harming them. Students can ask questions like: (1) What was the offense and how did you feel as a result? (2) How did you overcome your negative feelings towards the person? (3) How did you forgive the person? (4) What advice do you have about forgiving others? Students write an essay about their findings.

Learning from elders about repentance. Students interview elders about a situation in which the elder repented after hurting someone. Students can ask questions like: (1) What was the offense and how did the person feel as a result? (2) How did you overcome your negative feelings towards the person? (3) Did you do anything to show your repentance? (4) What advice do you have about repenting? Students write an essay about their findings.

What if I caused a negative consequence? Discuss ways that students can make amends for causing harm. Situations you might discuss include (a) immediate consequences to someone (e.g., loss of property, physical injury); (b) delayed consequences (e.g., wasting water uses up what is available); (c) long-term consequences (e.g., psychological harm of bullying); (d) combination of consequences (e.g., burning leaves creates an immediate hazard, delayed health consequences from breathing the air, long-term consequences for air pollution and global warming).

Changing your heart after hurting someone. Sometimes we hurt others impulsively, without thinking. We react angrily to a perceived threat or slight. We must learn to take the perspective of the other and feel empathy for them. Have students read several scenarios describing one person hurting another. Have students discuss (a) How did each person feel before, during and after the confrontation? (b) How should each person change their thinking and their hearts to feel positively towards the other?

Resolving Conflicts by Making Amends
Ideas for Developing Skills

Level 2 (continued)

Discriminating forgiveness from being a doormat. Show examples of true forgiveness (e.g., Nelson Mandela) and examples of a person being unassertive in front of a powerful person (e.g., a battered woman who keeps 'forgiving' her partner and returning to him).

How to apologize (Forni, 2002). Discuss the proper way to apologize: (1) You must know exactly what you did wrong; (2) you must understand the effect of your action; (3) you must not look for excuses; (4) don't use a pseudo-apology like "I know how you feel," "I see where you are coming from," "I'm sorry you feel that way," or "I'm trying to correct the situation"; (5) remember that an apology is not an authorization to be inconsiderate; (6) remember that the person may need some time to forgive you. Continuing your improved behavior, you may apologize again at a later date.

Level 3: Practice Procedures
Set goals, Plan steps of problem solving, Practice skills

Attitude Identification. In discussing a family or community story about a grudge, the class identifies ways the participants' thinking could have fostered forgiveness.

Practice forgiveness. Practice steps of forgiveness on behalf of a story character or on a small personal hurt.

Restorative justice in the classroom. Practice the restorative justice approach when a severe conflict arises among students.

Changing history. Students find conflicts in historical readings. They discuss what forgiveness would have looked like and have made a difference had it been granted.

A repentance and forgiving lifestyle. Students find examples of people who live forgiveness and repentance on a daily basis. How are their lives different? What do they do differently?

Resolving Conflicts by Making Amends
Ideas for Developing Skills

Level 4: Integrate Knowledge and Procedures
Execute plans, Solve problems

Student stories of forgiveness. Students write a story about forgiving someone and/or a story about being forgiven. They should describe how forgiveness was communicated, how each person felt, and what happened to the relationship.

Journal. Students reflect and write on personal experiences with grudges and forgiveness for one week. Students should describe what happened, how they felt, what they did, and whether or not they forgave or held a grudge. **Assess** writing.

Step #8: Making amends. Alcoholics Anonymous has 12-steps for recovering addicts to complete. Step Eight is making a list of everyone the person has ever hurt (and how) and then making respectful amends in some way (e.g., apologizing face to face, writing a letter to a deceased person, performing a ritual in the honor of the person—like planting a tree). Have students make confidential lists of the people they have harmed. Then have them make and carry out a plan for making amends to at least one of the people. Encourage them to report to the class if they feel comfortable.

Assessment Hints

Make Amends

Use role play to assess skills in apologizing.

Use essays about historical or literary figures.

Use journaling to gauge progress in self-awareness.

Create a Climate
to Develop Skills for Resolving Conflicts and Problems

- Use conflict resolution and negotiation strategies to solve classroom conflicts.
- Discourage any form of violence in the classroom (e.g., putdowns, hostility).
- Use class meetings. The purpose of the meeting is to set goals and rules together, negotiate, and resolve problems, and to give students the opportunity to practice communication and conflict resolution. The teacher should play a mediating or facilitating role in the class meeting but should not direct it. The students should be allowed this time to practice leadership and politeness skills as well. See Lickona's (1991) *Educating for Character*, pp. 139-160, for more strategies and ideas for class meetings.

Sample Student Self-Monitoring
Resolving Conflict and Problems

⭕	**Negotiate**
	I can change my position without compromising my ethical ideas in order to reach an agreement.
	I can negotiate a conflict using several steps.
	Interpersonal Problem Solving
	I can resist peer pressure.
⭕	I can think for myself.
	I know steps to solving a problem.
	Make Amends
	I have apologized sincerely.
	I know exactly what I did.
	I know what effect my action had.
⭕	I feel empathy for the person I harmed.
	I have not made an excuse for myself.
	I have made it up to the person.

Post These Attitudes Regarding Violence
(Prothrow-Stith & Weissman, 1991, p. 173)

1. Violence should not be considered in resolving conflict with others.
2. Conflict is a normal part of human interaction.
3. When people take the time to know themselves and their perspectives on subjects relative to the situation, they can learn how to get along with others who have different perspectives.
4. Most disputes do not have to have a winner or loser (win/win is the ideal solution).
5. Individuals who learn to be assertive, non-violently, can avoid becoming victims or bullies.

PHASES OF FORGIVENESS
(Enright, 2001)

PHASE 1: Uncovering your anger
How have you avoided dealing with anger?
Have you faced your anger?
Are you afraid to expose your shame or guilt?
Has your anger affected your health?
Have you been obsessed about the injury or the offender?
Do you compare your situation with that of the offender?
Has the injury caused a permanent change in your life?
Has the injury changed your worldview?

PHASE 2: Deciding to forgive
Decide that what you have been doing hasn't worked.
Be willing to begin the forgiveness process.
Decide to forgive.

PHASE 3: Working on forgiveness
Work toward understanding.
Work toward compassion.
Accept the pain.
Give the offender a gift.

PHASE 4: Discovery and release from emotional prison
Discover the meaning of suffering.
Discover your need for forgiveness.
Discover that you are not alone.
Discover the purpose of your life.
Discover the freedom of forgiveness.

EA-1 Resolving Conflicts and Problems

Ethical Action 2

Asserting Respectfully
(Act Assertively)

According to Alberti and Emmons (1975), assertive behavior is choosing for oneself (not for others and not others for self); it is expressive (not inhibited, and not depreciative of others); self-enhancing (but not at the expense of another); and can help in achieving a desired goal (but not by hurting others).

WHAT

Assertive behavior is exerting oneself to achieve a desired goal through constructive interaction with others. On a continuum, assertiveness lies between passiveness (doing for others at the expense of achieving one's own goals) and aggressiveness (achieving one's goals at the expense of others). Assertiveness skills should be used to speak up for the needs of others. When you speak up for someone's needs, you want to persuade your audience. Persuasion skills must be used carefully so as to respect the rights and responsibilities of the listener.

WHY

Standing up for oneself or for others in a non-aggressive but non-passive manner is a responsible action that prevents bullying or victimization. If a person does not stand up to a bully, the bully will not only hurt that person but continue to hurt others. Everyone has needs that are expressed and require satisfaction (e.g., eating, having friends). People who are assertive about their needs can avoid becoming victims or bullies in order to get their needs met. Children who are assertive and competent are, in fact, more prosocial (Eisenberg & Mussen, 1989).

SUBSKILLS OVERVIEW
Attend to human needs
Build assertiveness skills
Use rhetoric respectfully

Web Wise
The World Bank has information resources on a variety of human needs and problems:
    http://youthink.worldbank.org/4kids
See www.moralintelligence.com for quizzes on bullyproofing and other quizzes and information.

Asserting Respectfully by Attending to Human Needs

Ralph Nader has been an advocate for consumers for decades. He has spoken up about the dangers of particular products to people and helped initiate safety standards in many areas.

Creative and Expert Implementer Real-Life Example

Ideas for Developing Skills

Level 1: Immersion in Examples and Opportunities
Attend to the big picture, Learn to recognize basic patterns

Humans, other animals, plants. Compare and contrast the needs of plants, humans, and other animals and how each tries to meet their needs. ★

What children need. Students read about child development, watch films of young children and identify what needs drive their actions. What is the source of each need?

Identify daily needs. Students interview a family member about what needs they have each day and how they meet them. **Assess** with journaling and reporting to class.

Identify personal needs. Students keep track of a day in their lives according to what needs they have and how they meet them. Which are needs for life? Which are needs for social status? Which needs could they give up?

THE PROCESS FOR LEARNING ASSERTIVENESS
(Alberti & Emmons, 1974)

1. Observe your behavior
2. Keep a log (of your assertiveness)
3. Concentrate on a particular situation
4. Review your responses
5. Observe an effective model
6. Imagine yourself handling the situation
7. Try it out
8. Get feedback
9. Repeat 7-9 until ready for 10
10. Do it in the real situation

EA-2 Asserting Respectfully

Starred ★ activities within each subskill go together!

Asserting Respectfully
by Attending to Human Needs
Ideas for Developing Skills

Level 2: Attention to Facts and Skills
Focus on detail and prototypical examples, Build knowledge

Basic human needs. Discuss what humans need.

1. To start a discussion, use Abraham Maslow's (1943) theoretical idea about a human hierarchy of needs (see the Appendix). Have students identify how a favorite character (book or TV) has their needs in each category met. If they are not being met, have students identify ways to get the needs met.

2. Identify needs of individuals and groups in the community. Have students identify how a favorite character fulfills their needs in each category. If they are not being met, have students identify ways to get the needs met.

3. Students interview a community member and discuss Maslow's hierarchy. The community member identifies areas in which community members' needs are not being met. The student and community member identify ways to meet the needs.

Perspectives on needs. Give students scenarios for role play that encourage perspective taking and understanding others' needs, for example: (1) student has become paralyzed in both legs; (2) student has no home and no money; (3) student cannot speak English.

Needs of the poor. Study poverty in one of the following ways with a culminating activity in which students create an artistic representation, poem, song, essay, or play about poverty. (1) Invite a local community leader who works with the poor. Ask the speaker to help the students understand what a poor person has to deal with on a daily basis. (2) Do web research on poverty and its effects on daily life. Explore organizational websites of those who work with the poor, nationally or internationally. (3) Use an exercise illustrating world hunger and discuss what might be done to make things more fair (e.g., distributing food according to population distribution in the world).

Level 3: Practice Procedures
Set goals, Plan steps of problem solving, Practice skills

Needs of 'out' groups. Have students identify local community groups they feel are very different from themselves. Identify what needs people in these groups have. Identify situations that are beneficial to the students' groups but harmful to these out-groups.

EA-2 Asserting Respectfully

Starred activities within each subskill go together!

Asserting Respectfully
by Attending to Human Needs
Ideas for Developing Skills

Starred ★ activities within each subskill go together!

Level 3 (continued)

Asking for help. Discuss how to ask for help in different situations. For example, ask for an explanation if you don't understand something. Practice.

Rejection situations. Students identify a situation at school where some children are rejected.

Positive styles across cultures. In order to build cross-cultural skills, practice different styles of communicating: (1) personal needs, (2) group needs, (3) needs of strangers, and (4) citizen needs.

Level 4: Integrate Knowledge and Procedures
Execute plans, Solve problems

Balancing needs. Discuss how social interaction is a constant balance of personal needs/goals vs. the needs/goals of others. Have students keep a journal for a week about how they do this and discuss how to do it in different ways.

Speaking up for a victim. Discuss how to intervene assertively to help someone (1) who is being picked on; (2) who is not getting the attention they need; (3) who is being gossiped about. Practice with role play. Then implement in real life and report.

Volunteer. Have students volunteer at a local social service agency. They should keep track of all the human needs that are presented, the ones the agency tries to alleviate, and the ones it cannot or does not. Ask the students to participate in helping and to report on the experience.

Assessment Hints

Attend to Human Needs

Use multiple-choice, true-false, short answer, or essay tests to assess student knowledge about how to identify needs or common needs of humans, communities, families.

Have students keep a journal of their own, family's, or community's needs and assess the journal entries.

Have students write reports on their records of needs and present them to class.

Have students role play scenarios and demonstrate behaviors of identifying needs.

EA-2 Asserting Respectfully

To better identify needs and act assertively, pay attention to these communication channels:

Eye contact

Content of what you expressing

Congruent facial expressions

Voice tone, inflection, volume

Timing

Gestures

Body posture

Asserting Respectfully by Building Assertiveness Skills

Creative and Expert Implementer Real-Life Example

Susan B. Anthony was an assertive activist for equal rights for women. She supported women's right to vote.

Rosa Parks took action and is remembered as a symbol of civil disobedience, taking an action that harms no one but refuses to give in to injustice.

Ideas for Developing Skills

Level 1: Immersion in Examples and Opportunities
Attend to the big picture, Learn to recognize basic patterns

⭐ **What is assertive?** Study the specific characteristics of assertive behavior: (1) Watch film/video clips of respectful, assertive behavior and discuss. (2) Discuss conflict situations that make both people feel good in the end.

Distinguish assertiveness from aggressiveness and passive aggressiveness. Show film clips or act out examples of these three types of behavior. Have students identify which is which.
(a) Examples of aggressiveness
- Fred takes Mark's pencil. Mark grabs it back and punches Fred.
- Samantha tells Dora that she can't borrow Samantha's bicycle. Dora throws down the bike.
- Luke doesn't want to try a cigarette from Beth. Beth tells him to beat it, that she doesn't want to go out with him anymore.

(b) Examples of passive aggressiveness
- Fred takes Mark's pencil. Later Mark makes a put-down remark about Fred.
- Samantha tells Dora that she can't borrow Samantha's bicycle. Dora later "forgets" to return Samantha's science book.
- Luke doesn't want to try a cigarette from Beth. Beth ignores him the next time they meet.

(c) Examples of assertiveness
- Fred takes Mark's pencil. Mark tells Fred he wants it back.
- Samantha tells Dora that she can't borrow Samantha's bicycle. Dora says, "I need to get to the drug store quickly to pick up a prescription for my mom. Are you sure I can't use it for that?"
- Luke doesn't want to try a cigarette from Beth. Beth says, "I'm really disappointed in you."

EA-2 Asserting Respectfully

Starred ⭐ activities within each subskill go together!

Asserting Respectfully
by Building Assertiveness Skills
Ideas for Developing Skills

Level 2: Attention to Facts and Skills
Focus on detail and prototypical examples, Build knowledge

Contexts for assertiveness. (1) Day to day: Students find examples of assertiveness in their daily contexts. (2) Working with classmates: Students discuss how to be assertive when working in a classroom group. (3) Expressing anger: Students discuss how to express anger assertively.

Analyzing scenarios for assertiveness. According to Seligman (1995), there are four things that constitute assertiveness. Ask the students to identify these four things in scenarios.
1. Describe the situation that is upsetting, without blaming or getting emotional.
2. Tell other person your feelings.
3. Tell other person what you want him to change.
4. Tell other person how the change would make you feel.

Counteracting teasing (Borba, 1999). Have students calmly practice each of the following strategies in response to teasing from a partner or group. The respondent needs to look strong (have the partner or group help with this), look the teaser in the eye and use a strong voice. No teasing back!
1. Assert yourself by naming the behavior and telling the aggressor to stop (e.g., "Teasing is mean so stop it.").
2. Respond to an insult with a non-defensive question like "Why do you want to say that?"
3. Tell the person what you want them to do (e.g., "I want you to leave me alone").
4. Agree with the teaser lightheartedly.
5. Ignore the teasing.
6. Respond to each tease with a reply but don't let the teasing get to you. For example, "Gee, thanks for telling me." "So what?" (Frankel, 1996).

Level 3: Practice Procedures
Set goals, Plan steps of problem solving, Practice skills

Practice assertiveness in different contexts.
1. Assertiveness in different cultures. Students gather information about how people are assertive in the cultures of their community. Students share this information with classmates in reports and skits. Students practice different ways of being assertive.
2. Help younger children with refusal skills. Students learn about internal and external pressures to use chemical substances and develop methods and reasons to counter these. They present skits based on their knowledge to younger children.

EA-2 Asserting Respectfully

Starred ⭐ activities
within each subskill
go together!

Asserting Respectfully
by Building Assertiveness Skills
Ideas for Developing Skills

Level 3 (continued)

Practice the steps of assertiveness. Students practice acting out the four steps of assertiveness with scenarios in which they need to be assertive. For example:
(1) Your dad sometimes calls you "Squirt" and other nicknames in front of your friends and it bothers you.
(2) Your mom has been yelling at you a lot lately for little things you've done wrong. You feel sad when she yells at you and you wish she could tell you what was wrong without yelling at you.
(3) A kid from the high school asks if you want to try some pot. He calls you "chicken." You don't want to try the pot and you're annoyed that he's asking you.
(4) A boy took your homework and handed it in as his. Confront the student.

Practice assertiveness in complex interactions.
(1) Conversation. Students start a conversation with a stranger and maintain the conversation.
(2) Returns. Students act out returning faulty items to a store.
(3) Request for behavior changes. Students act out asking someone to turn down a stereo at a park or to stop talking in a movie theatre.
(4) Standing up for yourself.
Students act out a conversation with someone
who insists that they are right.
(5) Asking for a date. Students act out asking for a date (phone, in person).
(6) Public speaking. Students give a short speech in front of a group.

Changing your behavior instead of complaining (based on Forni, 2002). If you find yourself wanting to complain about things, make sure that you are not just distracting yourself from dissatisfaction with the way you are handling your life. Then examine what you could do differently to make yourself more content. Discuss situations where a complaint can be handled by changing your own behavior. For example: (a) A person sits next to you on the bus who is wearing so much perfume it makes you ill. (b) A friend keeps criticizing your clothes. (c) Your little brother or sister keeps interrupting you when your friends are over. (d) The person you are sitting next to at lunch keeps whistling.

Express a complaint constructively (Gibbs, Potter, & Goldstein, 1995). Have students brainstorm a list of problems they have complaints about and then have them practice the steps of giving a constructive complaint. (1) Identify the problem and how you are feeling. (2) Plan what you will say, to whom, and when. When is a good time to bring it up? (3) State your complaint. Take responsibility for your part in the problem. (4) Make a constructive suggestion. (5) Reflect on how it went. Possible problems include (a) getting a lot of homework from one teacher; (b) your parents making your curfew earlier than you like; (c) the school hot lunch meal being cold.

Asserting Respectfully
by Building Assertiveness Skills
Ideas for Developing Skills

Level 3 (continued)

Peer pressure refusal (Kurtzman, 1998). Teacher should:
(1) Identify with the students some decisions they might have to make.
(2) Define peer pressure and give a couple of age-appropriate examples.
(3) Discuss typical statements that peers make and why they might be effective.
(4) Discuss what a good friend would advise vs. what a bad friend would advise.
(5) Discuss consequences of good and poor decisions.
(6) Discuss "who do I want to give control to?"—myself, peers, tobacco companies, etc.
(7) Saying "no" to peers can be hard so we need to practice different ways.

Students practice 3-step refusal process. (a) Check out the scene and apply the trouble rule: will you break a rule or a law? (b) Make a good decision (if it's risky, is it worth it?). (c) Act quickly to avoid trouble, using one of 10 options: (1) Say "no!" (2) Leave. (3) Ignore. (4) Make a joke. (5) Suggest a better idea. (6) Make an excuse. (7) Act shocked. (8) Use flattery. (9) Change the subject. (10) Return the challenge.

Resisting trouble and troublemakers. (1) Have students write down situations in which they are tempted to do things that are wrong or against the law, or in which they find it hard to say "no." Put these situations into a hat and have small groups select one and role play it in front of the class. (2) Teacher or student assigns half of a group to be troublemakers and half to be decision makers. Whisper a scenario to the trouble makers and let them begin the skit. Have the rest of the class evaluate how well the decision makers fend off the peer pressure and what approaches they used.

Level 4: Integrate Knowledge and Procedures
Execute plans, Solve problems

Class officer. Have students take on the role of a class officer (e.g., etiquette officer, conflict officer, cleanliness officer) in which they must confront their classmates about changing their (rude, offensive, littering) behavior. Rotate these jobs so everyone gets to practice.

Assertiveness consulting. Have students set up a service for other students on being assertive in which they help design a plan for being assertive in a difficult situation. This could also be a booth at a school fair.

Assessment Hints

Building Assertiveness Skills

Use multiple-choice, true-false, short answer, or essay tests to assess student knowledge about assertiveness and appropriate assertive behaviors.

Have students keep a journal of their own or others' assertive behaviors and assess the journal entries.

Have students write reports on their records of assertiveness examples and present them to class.

Present a written scenario of a situation and have students respond in writing about how they would apply assertive behaviors to the situation.

Have students role play scenarios and demonstrate assertive behaviors.

Starred ★ activities within each subskill go together!

EA-2 Asserting Respectfully

Asserting Respectfully by Using Rhetoric Respectfully

Through his famous speeches, **Martin Luther King, Jr.** used rhetoric respectfully in convincing many white U.S. Americans to take a stand on the issue of segregation.

Ideas for Developing Skills

Level 1: Immersion in Examples and Opportunities
Attend to the big picture, Learn to recognize basic patterns

Behavior choices. Distinguish among styles of communicating: types that are passive, aggressive, or assertive.
> *Passive* behavior is doing things for others at the expense of oneself or achieving one's own goals.
> *Aggressive* behavior is achieving one's goals at the expense of others, their goals or well-being.
> *Assertive* behavior is choosing for oneself, not choosing for others and not others choosing for self; assertive behavior is expressive (not inhibited, and not depreciative of others); assertive behavior is self-enhancing (but not at the expense of another) and can help in achieving a desired goal (but not by hurting others).

(1) Discuss film clips of people communicating. Identify which communications are assertive, passive and aggressive. (2) Watch and read stories about the consequences for acting aggressively, assertively or passively.

Respectful disagreement. Show examples of people who respectfully disagree with others. Characteristics include focusing on principles of respect towards the opponent (following the golden rule of treating them as you wish to be treated), focus on the issue and justifications for your position, not on criticizing the opponent, using reasoning and not coercion (e.g., threats or whining). Have students keep track of the characteristics.

Disrespectful disagreement. Show examples of disrespectful disagreement. These examples will include such things as: Using dramatic examples and exaggerations to snow the opponent, badmouthing whoever disagrees with you (e.g., calling them evil or making fun of some personal characteristic) instead of dealing with the issue.

How to persuade and how not to. Show examples of people who try to persuade respectfully. Contrast these with examples of disrespectful persuading (e.g., attacking the other person, using alarming rhetoric, taking resistance personally).

Starred ★ activities within each subskill go together!

Asserting Respectfully
by Using Rhetoric Respectfully
Ideas for Developing Skills

Level 1 (continued)

Leaders who disagree respectfully. Bring in a community leader known for their respectful disagreements with others. Have the students devise questions for the speaker (e.g., what do you think is respectful when you talk to another person? What do you do when you are angry with the person?).

Level 2: Attention to Facts and Skills
Focus on detail and prototypical examples, Build knowledge

Distinguish modes in contexts. Distinguish among passive, aggressive, and assertive behaviors: (1) Students find and identify characteristics of different styles in favorite television shows. (2) Students find and identify the different styles in the news. (3) Students identify the common approaches in the students' cultures.

Cultural differences in assertiveness. Discuss the different ways cultures express assertively (1) needs, (2) authority and strength, (3) knowledge, (4) anger, (5) confusion, (6) saying no politely. Have students find examples in stories, news, TV and bring to class.

Give constructive criticism (Forni, 2002). Constructive criticism focuses on an issue (not the person), an observation (not accusation), shows empathy (it's happened to me), suggests a solution, and ends on a positive note. Have students practice constructive criticism and coach each other.

Civil arguments. Have students investigate and find examples of civil disagreements. What are the characteristics of these arguments? Have them present their findings to the class in a report, poster, or role play.

Respectful interactions. Friel and Friel (2000) say that sometimes people think that the best way to relate to another person is to argue or pick a fight and act tough. This approach turns most people off and is generally harmful to relationships. If you find yourself in a situation where the other person is acting this way, you can keep from falling into the trap of arguing and maintain your dignity: (a) Don't take the bait to counterargue. (2) Somehow affirm the other person by saying, for example, "I see your point." (3) Steer the interaction into a conversation that you want to talk about. (4) Don't let the other person feel too uncomfortable. Set up easy responses at first.

Starred activities within each subskill go together!

Asserting Respectfully
by Using Rhetoric Respectfully
Ideas for Developing Skills

Level 3: Practice Procedures
Set goals, Plan steps of problem solving, Practice skills

Peer relations. Students come up with and demonstrate ways to respond respectfully in several kinds of situations. Students distinguish between passive, aggressive and assertive responses. Types of situations can include: (a) In same-age project, students reflect on how to respond to a peer who is uncooperative. (b) Teammate is forgetting their responsibility. (c) Classmate doesn't return a favorite pen that was borrowed. (d) Friend arrives late to pick you up.

Respectful rhetoric against injustice. In 2002, Bob Herbert wrote several columns about injustice against innocent citizens in several states. Read several columns and have students discuss what kind of respectful intervention could be taken by citizens like themselves in situations like these. To find more examples like these check out the Southern Poverty Law Center website (www.splcenter.org).

Respectful rhetoric against drug use among adults. Role play students talking to adults about their overuse of drugs. What could the student say? How would it vary if the adult were a parent, an older sibling, a distant relative, a teacher, an acquaintance, a stranger?

Respectful rhetoric against environmental violation. Native Americans often speak about their concern for the well being of the earth. They tend to use respectful rhetoric, not demonizing those on the other side. Have students find examples of what Native Americans say (start with www.indians.org) and present it to class.

Respectful rhetoric for human rights. Have students investigate human rights as seen by an advocacy organization. How does the organization get its point across? Does it use respectful rhetoric? Sample organizations include Amnesty International (www. amnesty.org), which has a reputation for its respectful but firm and persistent voice for human rights around the world, the Anti-Defamation League (www.adl.org) which has materials to fight prejudice, UNICEF (www.unicef.org) which has put out the United Nations Convention on the Rights of the Child and a report on the status of children.

Starred activities
within each subskill
go together!

Asserting Respectfully
by Using Rhetoric Respectfully
Ideas for Developing Skills

Level 4: Integrate Knowledge and Procedures
Execute plans, Solve problems

Mentoring. In cross-age tutoring project, students reflect on how to respond to a tutee who is uncooperative. Students distinguish between passive, aggressive and assertive responses. ★

Give speeches by others. Have students find examples of respectful persuasive speeches (e.g., from Martin Luther King Jr., Gandhi, Gettysburg address), practice them and give them to the class.

Practice ethical persuasion. Pratkanis and Aronson (1992) identify several questions for determining whether or not a given message is ethical: (1) What are the goals of your message? Is it to mislead or for personal gain at the expense of truth? (2) What is the content of the message? Do you believe what you are saying? (3) Does the message induce thought or play on prejudices? Are you presenting the facts accurately? Or are you appealing to fear? Unethical persuasion appeals to our fears and emotions, oversimplifies the situation, misleads attention to focus on the viewpoint of the persuader. (4) Have students practice giving messages to each other that follow these principles. (5) Have students write a persuasive speech about a critical issue in a domain (e.g., science, business, education, arts, sport, politics) using respectful rhetoric.

Assessment Hints

Use Rhetoric Respectfully

Assess with multiple-choice scenarios: present a scenario and ask the students to select the passive response, the aggressive response and the assertive response.

Use true-false, short answer, or essay tests to assess student knowledge about different communication styles.

Present a written scenario or video clip of different situations and have students respond in writing what an aggressive, passive, or assertive response would be.

Have students role play scenarios and demonstrate culturally appropriate communication styles.

Assess journal entries when journaling is a part of the activity.

Starred ★ activities within each subskill go together!

Create a Climate
to Cultivate Respectful Assertiveness

Generally:

Provide a means for students to raise issues of concern.

Provide a means for students to raise issues of concern with each other.

Encourage students to use I statements with each other.

("I feel_____ when _____ because ___")

Promote Student Decision Making. Students can be involved in making decisions about the following:

(1) Materials and procedures to use in accomplishing assignments

(2) Supplementary content to learn

(3) Classroom rules

(4) Where to sit

(5) How to form work groups

(6) Order of task accomplishment

(7) Assignments

(8) School-wide rules and policies

Sample Student Self-Monitoring
Asserting Respectfully
Encourage active learning by having students learn to monitor their own learning

Attend to human needs
I pay attention to what I'm feeling.
I pay attention to what others are feeling and thinking.
I pay attention to what other people want.
I am sensitive to balancing the needs of others with my own needs.

Build assertiveness skills
I can question rules that seem unfair.
I can handle my peers teasing me.
I can ask for help when I need it (in class, at home).

Use rhetoric respectfully
I change my communication style according to the context.
I can adjust my communication style for different cultures.
I don't force my opinion on others.

Selections to Post in the Classroom
for Asserting Respectfully

Post the principles of assertive behavior
(Alberti & Emmons, 1974)

- It's important to distinguish between passive, aggressive, and assertive behavior.

- Relationships are always about sharing power.

- Non-assertiveness enables harmful behavior in others.

- You can change your attitude by changing your behavior first.

- Favors power sharing in relationships.

Taking Initiative as a Leader

(Be a Leader)

WHAT
Ethical character is manifested in good leaders as well as followers. An ethical leader will encourage or inspire others to follow their ethical instincts by encouraging these attitudes, knowledge and skills. Ethical leaders will modulate their form of leadership depending on the task at hand. They will also use the resources of the group to the greatest effect. Good leaders are able to mentor others in ethical leaderhip.

WHY
At one time or another, everyone becomes a leader. Leadership comes in many forms: Whether it is a friend making a suggesting to a friend, a sibling taking care of a younger sibling, or a classmate in charge of an activity. Sometimes people think that there is only one right way to lead or one type of ideal leader. It is important to be able to skillfully lead in different ways depending on the need and context.

SUBSKILLS OVERVIEW
Be a leader
Take initiative for and with others
Mentor others

Web Wise
Explore the quizzes at www.myskillsprofile.com for ideas about what different kinds of skills to work on
The Alberta Teacher's Association has a website with guidelines on mentoring:
http://www.teachers.ab.ca/pages/home.aspx
http://www.cep.unt.edu/novice.html
Developing student leadership:
http://www.casaa-resources.net/resources/sourcebook/student-leadership

Taking Initiative as a Leader by Being a Leader

Creative and Expert Implementer Real-Life Example

Cesar Chavez was an extremely effective leader for Chicano and Filipino agricultural workers from the 1950s until his death in 1993. He organized community and labor organizations for the agricultural workers and founded a union for them (National Farm Workers Association). He attracted national attention with his boycotts to raise awareness of the dangerous and harmful working conditions of the workers.

Ideas for Developing Skills

Level 1: Immersion in Examples and Opportunities
Attend to the big picture, Learn to recognize basic patterns

Defining leadership by reading stories. After reading a story about Harriet Tubman or a similar leadership figure, focus a large part of the discussion on leadership by having students brainstorm on what leadership means and recording responses on board or a poster. Next divide the class into groups and ask them to rank order the characteristics of leadership and then bring the groups together to arrive at a consensus. In this final phase, phrase words as qualities and ask students how these words could be useful to them. Ask each student to choose a person they feel is a leader and to quick-write for five minutes. Students can share their writing with the group and each group can pick one to share with the class. See Paul (1987) *Critical Thinking Handbook*, pp. 130-132, for more ideas.

Choice of leadership style. Discuss different kinds of leadership (e.g., authoritarian, autocratic, dictatorial). Have students identify these in current leaders.

How do kids lead? Present and discuss examples of leadership by young people. Find examples locally or from national organizations like: Kids for Saving Earth Worldwise (KSE, www.kidsforsavingearth.org, kseww@aol.com), Kids for a Clean Environment (KidsFACE, www.kidsface.org, kidsface@mindspring.com), Kids Against Pollution, Poverty & Prejudice (KAP, kidsagainstpollution.org, kap@borg.com), Natural Guard works with inner-city youth on community action projects (tng@snet.net).

Starred ★ activities within each subskill go together!

Taking Initiative as a Leader by Being a Leader
Ideas for Developing Skills

Level 2: Attention to Facts and Skills
Focus on detail and prototypical examples, Build knowledge

Effective leadership. Identify effective task and social leadership skills and how situations can determine what kind of leadership is needed. Have students identify the goals and effects of different leaders in history.

Challenges of leadership. Discuss with the students the impediments to being a leader: embarrassment, not wanting to be different, thinking others will do it. Study examples in stories or history of people who were not impeded.

Examine the process of leadership. Have students select from a list of leaders (historical or current). These can be political, civic, business, activist, artistic, research, scientific, technological (e.g., inventors), academic, or cultural leaders. Students do one of the following and report on findings: (1) Read as much about the leader as possible to find out the leader's leadership style. What important decisions did the leader make? How did the leader change the world? (2) Shadow a local leader. Find out what a day is like, what decisions are made, what the leader does to stay focused, what the leader does to make sure decisions are ethical. (3) Identify the skills the leader has based on a list of character skills.

Communication skills of leaders. Have students practice important leadership skills such as (a) public speaking (e.g., clear expression, good opening, eye contact); (b) managing impressions (e.g., through clothes and grooming, body language, enunciation and accent, how to meet someone, how to make conversation); (c) setting personal goals (see Action Skill # 4).

Level 3: Practice Procedures
Set goals, Plan steps of problem solving, Practice skills

Identify a role model. Students select a good leader (who helped his or her entire people) and write about how they could imitate that leader in their daily life. Then have them implement their plan and report on it.

Find a problem. Students identify a local problem, find out as much as possible about it, generate solutions for how to remedy it.

Starred activities within each subskill go together!

Taking Initiative as a Leader by Being a Leader
Ideas for Developing Skills

Level 4: Integrate Knowledge and Procedures
Execute plans, Solve problems

Being a leader. Cross-age tutoring is a situation where an older student can demonstrate leadership. For example, older students (e.g., Grades 7 & 6) work with younger students (e.g., Grades 3 and 4) on homework or a community service project. See the Appendix (p. 143) for instructions.

Inspire others. Students practice techniques for helping others get motivated to take ethical action. According to Gladwell (2002) in *The Tipping Point*, there are three things that come together to make social change: (a) motivating the persons who are messengers to others, (b) making a message that sticks in people's minds, (c) changing the context so it supports or stimulates the behavior you want.

Give advocacy speeches. Have students develop advocacy speeches to persuade an audience to support a change that will help the community. The speakers should remember to: welcome the audience; connect with the audience; maintain eye contact; mean what you say; tell the audience what you are going to say, say it, and tell them what you said; make several clear points.

Assessment Hints

Be a Leader

Use multiple-choice, true-false, short answer, or essay tests to assess student knowledge about leadership styles, challenges to leadership, etc.

Use a real-life biography of a well known leader and have students describe the person's leadership style and leadership characteristics.

Have students role play scenarios and demonstrate leadership behaviors.

Starred ★ activities
within each subskill
go together!

Taking Initiative as a Leader by Taking Initiative for and with Others

In 1964, President **Lyndon B. Johnson** forcefully pushed the Civil Rights Act through Congress and signed the bill into law, against the wishes of some congressional representatives. He knew that this would alienate some Southern Democrats and it did. More important than state politics however was the fact that, with the Civil Rights Act, blacks calling for equal rights in states where they had been treated unfairly now had the federal law behind them.

Creative and Expert Implementer Real-Life Example

Ideas for Developing Skills

Level 1: Immersion in Examples and Opportunities
Attend to the big picture, Learn to recognize basic patterns

Leaders who helped others. Read stories about social leaders who helped their communities and discuss what would have happened without them.

Self-sacrifice. Read stories about social leaders who helped their communities at personal cost.

Family decisions. Discuss the different ways families make decisions.

Decisions with friends. Discuss ways people make decisions with their friends.

Community decisions. Watch an example of community decision making.

Level 2: Attention to Facts and Skills
Focus on detail and prototypical examples, Build knowledge

Local leaders. Invite local community members who have been active in speaking up for the disadvantaged. Ask them about their challenges and necessary skills.

Finding out about family decision making. Students interview their parents or other adults about how they make decisions in their families. Report to class and discuss the differences and options people have.

Finding out about decision making with friends. Students talk to older students about how they make decisions with their friends. Report to class and discuss the differences and options people have.

Taking Initiative as a Leader
by Taking Initiative for and with Others
Ideas for Developing Skills

Level 2 (continued)

Finding out about community decision making. Students interview community decision makers about how they make decisions for the community. Report to class and discuss the differences and options people have.

Level 3: Practice Procedures
Set goals, Plan steps of problem solving, Practice skills

Social action. Students work in groups to initiate social action. They can choose a social problem to work on over the semester. The teacher and group members evaluate the leadership style of each group member (see descriptions of leadership styles at http://www.casaa-resources.net/resources/sourcebook/student-leadership/leadership-styles.html or in Sisk and Rosselli's (1987) *Leadership: A Special Type of Giftedness*). (Example: Students may choose to create a recreation center in town for at-risk students where they have access to social services. They might work with the town board, write petitions, and lobby public officials. They may write grants, organize committees, and conduct opinion polls.)

Role play leader decision making. Students practice skills in ethical leadership (like listening, making a decision with everyone's welfare in mind, etc.). Assess with written responses to scenarios. Students take on the role of leader and decide what next steps to take.

Taking initiative for the common good. Students brainstorm about current needs in the classroom, school, or community. Have someone from the community come in and talk with students about service, sharing their stories and experiences. Students perform some school, civic, or humanitarian service.

Practice group decision making. Maier (1963) and Turner and Pratkanis (1994) have six suggestions for group decision making that have been shown to increase critical thinking and avoid the pitfalls of groupthink (where the group agrees without critical thinking): (1) Don't accept the first answer that comes up. Explore alternatives. (2) Keep focused on solving the problem, not criticizing other people or their ideas. (3) Keep track of all suggestions so that each can be fully explored. (4) Select a set of options and ask evaluative questions (e.g., What would that mean? What would happen if we did that?). (5) Protect people from individual attacks, especially those expressing minority opinions. (6) Make one of your goals understanding and resolving the differences of opinion in the group. Have students lead one another in decision making. Have them practice until they can master the procedures.

Starred ★ activities within each subskill go together!

Taking Initiative as a Leader
by Taking Initiative for and with Others
Ideas for Developing Skills

Level 3 (continued)

Decision-making in class meetings (Lickona, 1991). Facilitate class meetings led by teachers, usually 10 to 30 minutes long, on a consistent basis. Specifically, sticky situations type of class meetings help students work through difficult situations, enabling them to develop skills for real situations, including the ego-strength to do the right thing.

Level 4: Integrate Knowledge and Procedures
Execute plans, Solve problems

Weekly reports on taking initiative. Initiate weekly reporting on student activism. Have students decide what kind of unfairness they can address during the week and return the following week with a description of how they did so (alone or in groups).

Imitate ethical decision making in leaders. Students imitate a leadership style in leading a project. Afterwards, they reflect on and write about their experiences.

Becoming a community leader. Discuss with students how to get involved (1) in school governance and other activities by sharing information about what is available in the school and (2) in the community (civic, humanitarian).

Lead in taking social action. Have students take action in their community. Use the steps suggested by Lewis' (1998) *Kid's Guide to Social Action* (written for kids to use with worksheets and concrete guidelines): (1) Choose a problem in the neighborhood (Does an area feel unsafe? Smell bad? Look terrible? Are there needy people?). (2) Do your research (How do community members feel about the problem? What is the history of the problem). (3) Brainstorm possible solutions and choose the one that seems most possible and will make the most difference. (4) Build coalitions of support. Find all the people that agree with you (neighborhood, community, city, state, businesses, agencies). (5) Figure out (with the help of your coalition) who is your opposition and work with them on overcoming their objections. (6) Advertise (send out a news release, call tv, radio, newspaper reporters, churches). (7) Raise money if you need to. (8) Carry out your solution. Make a list of the steps you need to take (e.g., write letters, give speeches, pass petitions). (9) Evaluate and reflect on whether the plan is working. Did you try everything? Should you change something? Celebrate what you have done by writing about it, dramatizing it, drawing it. (10) Don't give up. Find the thing that will work.

Starred ★ activities within each subskill go together!

Assessment Hints

Take Initiative for and with Others

Use multiple-choice, true-false, short answer, or essay tests to assess student knowledge about skills for initiating social action.

Have students write reports on their initiation of social action (Level 3 & 4 activities).

Have students keep a journal of their social activism (Level 4 activity); assess their journal entries.

Have students role play scenarios and demonstrate behaviors taking initiative.

Taking Initiative as a Leader by Mentoring Others

Archie Manning, the father of Peyton Manning, talented quarterback of the Indianapolis Colts, was himself a great college and professional quarterback. He has instilled in his son not only his skill and love for the game, but also an integrity and commitment that Peyton exemplifies.

Ideas for Developing Skills

Level 1: Immersion in Examples and Opportunities
Attend to the big picture, Learn to recognize basic patterns

What do mentors do? Students find a mentor (of someone else) whom they can follow around to observe what a mentor does. **Assess** with a report on what they've observed.

What is a mentor? (1) Have the students interview older students and adults to find out what they think a mentor is. Ask those whom they interview who have been mentors for them. **Assess** with report on interview. (2) Have the students conduct research about what a mentor is and does. Encourage them to consider all of the people in theirlives who have been mentors for them. **Assess** participation in class discussion.

Level 2: Attention to Facts and Skills
Focus on detail and prototypical knowledge, Build knowledge

Ethical role model. Students are encouraged to be in contact with a mentoring role model. Optimally, this role model would be similar in many respects to the students (age, gender), yet have higher status (is considered "cool") and perform actions in situations that are similar to the ones the students face. **Assess** with a report on what the student learned.

Personal case of responsibility. Put the class in pairs and have the students exchange stories about times when they had to take responsibility for mentoring another. The partner of each student presents that student's mentoring experience to the class. **Assess** presentation to the class.

Being mentored. Students look at the people who give them advice (mentors) in their lives (including parents and teachers) and determine how the mentors guide them. **Assess** participation in class discussion.

Starred ⭐ activities
within each subskill
go together!

Interview a mentor. Interview people involved in actual mentor organizations (e.g. Big Brother, Big Sister). What compels them to be a mentor? What benefit do they gain by giving their time and energy in this way? **Assess** with report on interview.

Taking Initiative as a Leader by Mentoring Others
Ideas for Developing Skills

Level 3: Practice Procedures
Set goals, Plan steps of problem solving, Practice skills

Mentoring as a Big Brother/Big Sister (Dotson & Dotson, 1997). Invite a speaker from the Big Brother/Big Sister program to discuss the program with your students. Ask the speaker to emphasize the importance of good mentoring to the success of this program. Provide information about how your students can become involved with this program if they are interested. **Assess** with a report on what they've learned.

Mentoring in informal ways. Though there are formal roles of mentors, much of mentoring can (and often does!) occur in implicit ways, such as tutoring younger students, babysitting, or even just spending time with them. Children learn by modeling adolescents and adults, regardless of whether the child is in a formal mentoring relationship. Discuss how students can mentor younger students/ children informally by modeling appropriate behavior and then talking about it with the child.

Starred activities within each subskill go together!

Assessment Hints

Level 4: Integrate Knowledge and Procedures
Execute plans, Solve problems

Mentor Others

Mentoring a younger student. Pair students up with a younger student to meet once per week to work on a skill the older student can teach the younger student. **Assess** with a report on the experience by the student mentor.

Cross-age mentoring. Train student leaders (Grades 6 or 7) how to facilitate peer refusal; positive peer skills; and to present factual prevention information, including advertising and media techniques related to alcohol and tobacco, through puppet skits and role play activities to younger aged students (Grades 3 or 4). Mentoring younger students may instill a sense of duty to help others, especially those that are less developed or have fewer resources. Mentoring younger students may also facilitate the transition of focusing on external rewards for ethical behavior to having a more intrinsic satisfaction from helping.

Long-term mentoring. Have students take on a long-term mentoring job (e.g., semester long). This could be to help with (a) academics, (b) character skills, or (c) a short-term service project using activities from these books. The pairs should establish and keep track of goals. Request periodic reports. There should be a coach who can support and evaluate the success of the relationship.

Essays or Oral Reports. Have students write an essay or give an oral report about what they've learned about mentoring and who is a particularly good example of it in their lives.

Interview. Assess an interview by having the students report back to the class, either in a written report or orally, what they talked about and learned from the interview with one of their mentors.

Individual Performance. Following a cooperative or class activity or discussion targeting an issue related to mentoring, assess students on their individual contribution and performance.

Create a Climate
to Develop Taking Initiative as a Leader

- Set up opportunities for children to help one another.
- Set up rotating leadership roles in the classroom.
- When students have ideas for improving activities in the classroom, take them seriously.
- Offer examples of groups that help the poor and oppressed (e.g., Amnesty International, Oxfam) and design student projects to help.
- Give students an opportunity to make suggestions for structuring the classroom.*
- Give students opportunities to discuss all sides of controversial topics.*

*from Berman, 1997, pp. 108-109.

Promote positive attitudes
- The importance of practicing to be a leader to help others
- The importance of asking for help from one's family/community/affiliative group
- Everyone creates his or her own character

Help students realize their potential
- Ascribe students' prosocial behavior to their intrinsic motivation as much as possible
- Teach about the ways that individuals and groups influence the political process and make changes in society
- Teach structures and strategies
- Encourage independent thought and collaborative teamwork

Selections to Post in the Classroom
for Taking Initiative as a Leader

Emphasize the Characteristics of Positive Leadership
(Sisk & Rosselli, 1987)

- Listen to differing points of view for similarities and differences.
- Change one's own opinion if evidence points to a new way of thinking.
- Think in terms of hypothetical situations.
- Make peace during disagreements.
- Organize thoughts and provide cogent summaries.
- Be flexible to complete any task in order to complete a project.
- Meet deadlines.

Sample Student Self-Monitoring
Taking Initiative as a Leader

Encourage active learning by having students learn to monitor their own learning

○ **Be a Leader**

I want to make the world a better place.

I can make a quick decision when I have to.

I can organize my work.

I finish things by the time they are due.

I practice the skills of being a good leader.

I know different styles of leadership that I can choose from.

○ **Take Initiative for and with Others**

I want to help others.

I can help other people solve problems.

It is important to seek fair treatment of all people.

I can help others receive fair treatment.

I like to find out as much as I can about something before I
    make a decision.

I think about several options before I make a decision.

I can help my group get its work done.

I point out things that need to be done.

○ **Mentor Others**

I remember that I am a role model to younger children.

I recall how important mentors have been in my life.

I feel responsible for the person I am mentoring.

I am committed to helping the person I am mentoring.

Selections to Post in the Classroom
for Taking Initiative as a Leader

LEADERSHIP STYLES
Canadian Association of Student Activity Advisors
http: www.casaaleadership.ca

AUTOCRATIC
Bosses others around
Doesn't encourage discussion of ideas or new ways to do things
Doesn't encourage a feeling of teamwork
This style is effective when...
    When time is limited
    Group lacks knowledge and skills
    Group doesn't know each other
This style is ineffective when...
    When you want to develop a sense of team
    Members of group have knowledge or skills
    Group wants to be spontaneous or creative

LAISSEZ-FAIRE
Gives little or no direction
Offers opinion only when asked
Doesn't seem to be in charge
This style is effective when...
    The group is highly skilled and motivated
    The group has a sense of team
    The routines used are familiar to group members
This style is ineffective when...
    There is little team interdependence
    Team members have little knowledge or skill
    The group expects to be told what to do

DEMOCRATIC
Group members are involved in planning and doing
Asks for opinions first rather than telling people what to do
Encourages teamwork
This style is effective when...
    There is enough time
    The group is motivated or has a sense of team
    Group has skills or knowledge
This style is ineffective when...
    The group is not motivated
    Group has no knowledge or skills
    There is a lot of conflict among group members

Planning to Implement Decisions

(Plan action)

WHAT

Planning is a crucial step between making a judgment and carrying it out. In planning to implement an ethical decision, the student needs to think about what actions are required, possible obstacles, alternative actions, and resources that may be needed. Students need extensive practice in following through so that they can finely hone these skills and apply them in diverse situations.

WHY

Good planning skills are related to successful ethical implementation. Sometimes everything else goes right for an ethical action (e.g., noticing the problem, making a decision, being motivated to do it, having the resolve) but failure occurs in setting up the steps to complete an action.

SUBSKILLS

Think strategically
  Goals
  Actions to be taken to carry out decision
  Time, sequence, and locations of future actions
Implement successfully
  Avoiding obstacles
  Preparing alternative plans
Determine resource use
  What resources are needed to implement a plan
  How to find and obtain them

Web Wise

RETANET is the website for Resources for Teaching about the Americas which has lesson plans and links to use in many subjects: http://ladb.unm.edu/retanet/plans/attachments/
The East Asian Resources for Students and Teachers has lesson plans and other information for teachers: www.indiana.edu/~easc2/resources/#lessonplans

Creative and Expert Implementer Real-Life Example

Planning to Implement Decisions by Thinking Strategically

Herbert Hoover was an expert planner. As the 31st president of the United States, President Hoover took his beliefs about what the government's function should be and turned them into realities. Examples of his strategic thinking and excellent planning include the implementation of several programs to conserve of natural resources, protect equality of opportunity, encourage business efficiency, promote scientific research, and build major public works.

Ideas for Developing Skills

Level 1: Immersion in Examples and Opportunities
Attend to the big picture, Learn to recognize basic patterns

Awareness of planning. Over a week, point out situations that require thinking ahead. Include both explicit events, like taking a vacation or having a party, and implicit events, such as playing a game, dressing for school or completing school assignments. Discuss the sequence of actions people take to complete their goals (e.g., knowing action/event to be planned, knowing actions or steps that must take place to carry it out).

What planning looks like: Goals. Present students with various scenarios of planning (e.g., taking steps to build a homeless shelter), via written stories, videos, or a presentation by a community member, to describe the planning of a community event. Students discuss how strategic planning, with subgoals and concrete steps, is necessary for effectively implementing a decision or goal. Students also describe the sequence of actions for planning.

Planning in particular fields. Bring in one or more experts from the community (e.g., farmer, community organizer, engineer, sport player) to discuss and demonstrate how he or she uses planning in his or her work.

Level 2: Attention to Facts and Skills
Focus on detail and prototypical knowledge, Build knowledge

Attention to goals. In order to plan anything, one has to have a goal to plan towards it. Over a week, point out situations that require thinking ahead, and emphasize the goal of the planned event. After a number of examples, start asking students to identify the goal of the planned situation (rather than you explaining it to them). Then ask them to identify their own planning situations over a week and describe the planning situation and goal of the situation in a journal.

Starred ★ activities within each subskill go together!

Planning to Implement Decisions
by Thinking Strategically
Ideas for Developing Skills

Level 2 (continued)

Examples of strategic/nonstrategic thinking. Use books, movies, or television shows in which the characters show, or should have shown, strategic thinking. Discuss with students that planning involves identifying goals and the specific actions that need to be taken to implement these goals. Help students identify the character's goals and determine whether the character had to predict and plan actions to achieve his/her goals. Ask students to identify the actions that the character had to plan (or should have planned) to achieve his/her goals.

Observing planning. Have the students watch other people plan out loud. They could watch a teacher plan a party in class or a lesson for next week. They could also be assigned to watch their parent/guardian or community member plan an event (e.g., dinner, holiday event, family trip). Have the students write a description of the planning process, attending to goals, actions and sequence, of their family or community member.

Ethical planning at work. Have students visit and interview an adult at a job in which ethical decisions are made (i.e., human welfare is affected). Develop a set of questions about the ethical decisions on the job, such as what kinds of ethical decisions must be made, what kind of planning is done for each kind of ethical decision, which ones are more difficult and is there a special type of planning needed, etc. Students report to class.

Shadowing ethical planning. Have students observe an adult at work. Students should be prepared to write down what kinds of decisions were made, how they were planned, which decisions were ethical, etc. Students report to class.

Level 3: Practice Procedures
Set goals, Plan steps of problem solving, Practice skills

Strategic thinking in planning a class project: Goals and steps. In having students complete a big project for a class assignment, have part of the assignment be planning their project. Ask them to identify their goal in completing the project, specific actions that they need to take to achieve their goal, and a timeline for getting the actions done.

Planning an ethical decision: Planning sheet. Present students with an ethical dilemma in which they make a decision about what to do. Afterwards, ask students to plan how they would implement their decision. Have them use a personal planning sheet, in which they would describe in a table or algorithm: (1) their goal in resolving the dilemma, (2) specific actions that they need to take to achieve their goal, and (3) a timeline for getting the actions done.

Starred activities within each subskill go together!

Planning to Implement Decisions by Thinking Strategically
Ideas for Developing Skills

Level 4: Integrate Knowledge and Procedures
Execute plans, Solve problems

Thinking strategically about a future career: Goals. Ask students to identify what they would like their ideal career to be. Ask them to identify the *ultimate goal(s)* they would like to achieve in their career. Then have them describe what *actions* they would need to take to (1) be in the career and (2) achieve their career goal. Encourage them to consult people in their career of choice or find the information in interviews with career exemplars published in magazines or on the web.

Starred ★ activities within each subskill go together!

Thinking strategically about getting a part-time job: Strategies. Ask students to identify a part-time job that they would like to have during the summer or in high school. Have students identify what actions they would need to do to get the job (e.g., how and where would they look for their specified job, whether they would need any training or volunteer experience to qualify for the job, whether they would need to prepare an application or interview and how they would prepare for them, etc.). Have students then create a *timeline* that includes specific *steps* to get the job.

★ **Thinking strategically about a community problem: Goals and steps**. Present students with a community problem or issue. Ask students to come up with a solution to this problem (either individually, in groups, or as a class). Afterwards, ask students to plan how they would implement their decision. Have them write out a plan that includes: their *goal* in solving the problem, *specific actions* that they need to take to achieve their goal, and a *timeline* for getting the actions done. Have students present their plans to the class.

Assessment Hints

Think strategically

Use multiple-choice, true-false, short answer tests to assess students' knowledge of planning skills.

Present to students hypothetical scenarios of individuals partaking in planning and not planning for an activity. Ask the students to identify which scenarios had individuals who planned.

Have students write a report on their planning observations and hand it in to be assessed.

Give students a dilemma where the character has made a decision. Ask the students to describe the character's goal in implementing the decision, specific actions that the character needs to take to achieve their goal, and a timeline for getting the actions done.

Have students write an essay about their planning (for career or part-time job activities).

Planning to Implement Decisions by Implementing Successfully

Civil engineers are experts in planning. Constructing bridges across rivers and bays, engineers have to identify and overcome a multitude of obstacles in order to build safe bridges for thousands, possibly millions, of people to use. If their plans are not succesfully implemented, people's lives may be lost.

Creative and Expert Implementer Real-Life Example

Ideas for Developing Skills

Level 1: Immersion in Examples and Opportunities
Attend to the big picture, Learn to recognize basic patterns

What planning looks like: Avoiding failure. Present students with various scenarios of poor planning (e.g., having a birthday party for a friend and forgetting to buy a birthday cake and candles) and discuss what obstacles might have led to the bad outcome. Discuss with students how strategic planning needs to include thinking of possible obstacles ahead of time and having alternative plans for these obstacles. Students also describe what other possible obstacles could occur and alternative actions the character could take.

Level 2: Attention to Facts and Skills
Focus on detail and prototypical knowledge, Build knowledge

Examples of successful/unsuccessful implementation. Use books, movies, or television in which the characters show successful and unsuccessful implementation of goals. Discuss with students how the character did or did not implement his/her goal successfully. Emphasize the obstacles that arose and whether the character predicted these obstacles before they occurred. Also focus on the alternative plans that the character generated, or could have generated, to successfully implement his/her decision or goal.

Identifying obstacles in planning for a particular subject area. Ask students (or assist them) to select a goal in the subject matter. Plan the subgoals and steps to reach the subgoals and ultimately the overarching goal. Write these on a chart, and next to each step, write down possible obstacles and what might be done if they arise.

Identifying obstacles in ethical dilemmas. Present students with an ethical dilemma (could also be a community problem or issue). Ask students to come up with a solution to this problem, and have students resolve the dilemma or problem and identify the goal of their solution. Plan the subgoals and steps to reach them and the overarching goal. Write these on a chart, and next to each step, write down possible obstacles and what might be done if they arise.

Starred activities within each subskill go together!

Planning to Implement Decisions by Implementing Successfully
Ideas for Developing Skills

Assessment Hints

Implement successfully

Use multiple-choice, true-false, and short answer tests to assess students' knowledge of planning skills.

Present to students hypothetical scenarios of individuals partaking in unsuccessful and successful planning for an activity. Ask the students to identify which scenarios had individuals who exhibited successful and unsuccessful planning. Ask students to explain possible reasons about why the planning was unsuccessful.

Give students a dilemma where the character has made a decision. Ask the students to describe which obstacles the character may encounter and alternative plans to overcome the obstacles.

Have students record their planning and hand it in to be assessed.

Have students write an essay about their planning (for career or part-time job activities).

Level 3: Practice Procedures
Set goals, Plan steps of problem solving, Practice skills

Obstacle identification in planning a class project. In having students complete a big project for a class assignment, have part of the assignment be planning their project. Ask them to identify possible obstacles that may arise in completing their project and alternative actions to overcome the specified obstacles.

Planning an ethical decision: Plans for overcoming obstacles. Present students with an ethical dilemma (could also be a community problem or issue) in which they make a decision about what to do. Afterwards, ask students to plan how they would implement their decision. Have them use a personal planning sheet, in which they would describe in a table or algorithm: (1) possible obstacles that may arise in implementing their ethical decision, and (2) alternative actions to overcome the specified obstacles and successfully implement their decision.

Level 4: Integrate Knowledge and Procedures
Execute plans, Solve problems

Thinking strategically about a future career: Planning around obstacles. Ask students to identify what they would like their ideal career to be or a part-time job that they would like to have during the summer. Ask them to identify possible obstacles that could arise in attaining their career or part-time job and alternative actions that they could take to overcome the obstacles. Encourage them to consult people in their career of choice or find the information in interviews with career exemplars published in magazines or on the web.

Thinking strategically about a community problem: Planning around obstacles. Present students with a community problem or issue. Ask students to come up with a solution to this problem (either individually, in groups, or as a class). Afterwards, ask students to plan how they would implement their decision. Have them write out a plan that includes: possible obstacles that could arise and alternative actions that they could take to overcome the obstacles.

Starred ★ activities within each subskill go together!

Planning to Implement Decisions by Determining Resource Use

Assuring access for all patients needing organs for transplantation, the **United Network for Organ Sharing** (UNOS) developed and maintains the national patient waiting list for organ transplant. UNOS plays a critical role in determining resource (i.e., donated organ) use and distribution.

Creative and Expert Implementer Real-Life Example

Ideas for Developing Skills

Level 1: Immersion in Examples and Opportunities
Attend to the big picture, Learn to recognize basic patterns

What planning looks like: Resources. Present students with various scenarios of poor planning (e.g., having a birthday party for a friend and forgetting to buy a birthday cake and candles). Discuss with students how strategic planning needs to include thinking of all possible resources that will be needed and planning how much of the resources will be needed. Students also describe the possible resources may be needed for the example.

Level 2: Attention to Facts and Skills
Focus on detail and prototypical examples, Build knowledge

Identifying resources in a planning exercise. Ask students (or assist them) to select a goal in the subject matter. Plan the subgoals and steps to reach the subgoals and ultimately the overarching goal. Write these on a chart. Indicate what resources you will need for each step. Here is an example of resources needed for a lesson on communication skills:
1. <u>Semantic Knowledge Resources</u>: Using specific concepts, their principles, and associations to learn the skill (e.g., what "paraphrasing" means and when it should be used).
2. <u>Expertise Resources</u>: Hearing from an expert to learn about the skill (e.g., a news anchor from a local television station talks to students about the importance of speaking clearly and articulately).
3. <u>Procedural Knowledge Resources</u>: Using a specified procedure or process to learn the skill (e.g., the process of active listening).
4. <u>Material Resources</u>: Using concrete materials for the lesson (e.g., a video camera is used to tape student's speeches so that the student can self-evaluate his/her own speech).

EA-4 Planning to Implement Decisions

Starred ★ activities within each subskill go together!

Planning to Implement Decisions by Determining Resource Use
Ideas for Developing Skills

Level 2 (continued)

Identifying resources in ethical dilemmas. Present students with an ethical dilemma (could also be a community problem or issue). Ask students to come up with a solution to this problem, and have students resolve the dilemma or problem and identify the goal of their solution. Plan the sub-goals and steps to reach the subgoals and ultimately the overarching goal. Write these on a chart. Indicate what resources you will need for each step. Use the list on p. 92 or the "Linking to the Community" checklist (see Appendix) for ideas and to ensure comprehensiveness.

Level 3: Practice Procedures
Set goals, Plan steps of problem-solving, Practice skills

Identifying necessary resources for a class project. In having students complete a big project for a class assignment, have part of the assignment be planning their project. Ask them to identify all possible resources that they may need in completing their project and how they can obtain these resources.

Planning an ethical decision with resources in mind. Present students with an ethical dilemma (could also be a community problem or issue) in which they make a decision about what to do. Afterwards, ask students to plan how they would implement their decision. Have them use a personal planning sheet in which they would describe all possible resources that they may need in carrying out their decision and how they can obtain these resources.

Level 4: Integrate Knowledge and Procedures
Execute plans, Solve problems

Thinking strategically about a future career: Resources. Ask students to identify what they would like their ideal career to be. Ask them to identify all possible resources that may be needed in reaching their career and how they can access these resources. Encourage them to consult people in their career of choice or find the information in interviews with career exemplars published in magazines or on the web.

Thinking strategically about getting a part-time job: Resources. Ask students to identify a part-time job that they would like to have during the summer or in high school. Have students identify all possible resources that may be needed in being qualified for, finding out about jobs, and getting the job and how they can access these resources.

Starred activities within each subskill go together!

Planning to Implement Decisions by Determining Resource Use
Ideas for Developing Skills

Thinking strategically about a community problem: Resources.
Present students with a community problem or issue. Ask students to come
up with a solution to this problem (either individually, in groups, or as a
class). Afterwards, ask students to plan how they would implement their
decision. Have them write out a plan that includes all possible resources that
may be needed and how they can access these resources.

Assessment Hints

Determine resource use

Use multiple-choice, true-false, and short answer tests to assess
students' knowledge of planning skills.

Present to students hypothetical scenarios of individuals partaking in
unsuccessful and successful resource planning. Ask the students to
identify which scenarios had individuals who exhibited successful
and unsuccessful resource planning. Ask students to explain possible
reasons why the planning was unsuccessful.

Give students a dilemma where the character has made a decision.
Ask the students to describe what resources the character will/may
need and how the character could obtain the resources.

Have students record their resource planning and hand it in to be
assessed.

Have students write an essay about their resource planning (for
career or part-time job activities).

Starred activities
within each subskill
go together!

Examples of Resources

SOCIAL NETWORK RESOURCES
Family
Friendship
Service group
Neighborhood
Social groups
Community
City
Park & Rec
State
National
International

SEMANTIC KNOWLEDGE RESOURCES
Books and other library sources
Web
Librarians
Educators and Intellectuals
Business leaders
Community experts

AUTHORITY STRUCTURE RESOURCES
School officials
Government officials (all levels)
United Nations
Other Leaders

ORGANIZATIONAL RESOURCES
Any organization that can give guidance on your
problem/issue

PERSONAL RESOURCES
Abilities and skills that you have

AGE-GROUP RESOURCES
Teen groups in various community organizations
School groups
Senior Citizen groups
Children's groups
Women's groups
Men's groups

MATERIAL RESOURCES (types of materials)
Scraps (from scrap yards)
Second-hand (from second-hand stores, recycling
places)
New
Handmade

EXPERTISE RESOURCES
Social networking
Design
Musical
Physical (game/sport, dance)
Creating
Knowledge
Finance
Selling

FINANCIAL RESOURCES
Grants
Loans
Donors
Earn money
Bartering (exchanging one thing for another)

Create a Climate
to Develop Planning Skills

- Encourage students to carefully and systematically think about a plan before acting on the decision.
- Encourage students' commitment to knowing, using, and accessing resources when planning.

	# Sample Student Self-Monitoring ## Developing Planning Skills
	Encourage active learning by having students learn to monitor their own learning
○	
	Think strategically
	What are the goals of implementing ethical action?
	Did I identify all of the actions that are necessary to implement the decision?
	What is the sequence of future actions?
	What is the timeline for future actions?
	Where do the future actions need to take place?
○	**Implement successfully**
	Did I identify all of the possible obstacles that may arise when I am implementing the decision?
	Did I determine all of the alternative actions that I could take when faced with any one of the possible obstacles?
	Determine resource use
	Did I identify all of the resources that I could access to implement my decision?
○	Do I know how to access the resources I need?
	How should the resources be used?

Ethical Action 5

Cultivating Courage
(Develop Courage)

WHAT
Courage is using ethical integrity to stand-up for what you believe. Activities within and outside of the classroom are needed to (1) develop a sense of competence or self-efficacy, and to (2) reinforce the good feelings that can accompany taking risks for others.

WHY
Becoming knowledgeable in the other categories in the process of ethical action is a prerequisite for completing an ethical action, but knowledge alone is not sufficient to produce the desired behaviors in students. Students need to have courage to execute ethical actions and implement their beliefs.

SUBSKILLS OVERVIEW
Manage fear
Stand up under pressure
Manage change and uncertainty

Web Wise
This website has some interesting things to say about courage generally: http://www.geocities.com/cikusa/activist.html
See for information and lesson plans www.goodcharacter.com

Cultivating Courage
by Managing Fear

Earlier in his life, **Chris Carter** of the Vikings had a drug problem and little hope for himself. After his son was born, he got treatment for his drug problem and started life over. He became a leader among his teammates.

Creative and Expert Implementer Real-Life Example

Ideas for Developing Skills

Level 1: Immersion in Examples and Opportunities
Attend to the big picture, Learn to recognize basic patterns

Courage in stories. Students read stories of courage and discuss the courageous behavior and its implications for the hero or heroine. The following examples are from *A Call to Character* (Greer & Kohl, 1995):
1. An excerpt from Helen Keller's *The Story of My Life* is a story of Helen in a tree when a thunderstorm erupts. Helen describes how confronting and overcoming terror can lead to deep personal enrichment.
2. *Charlotte's Web* by E.B. White is a story of the intervention of Charlotte the spider to save her friend the pig when they learn he's being fattened for Christmas dinner. It demonstrates courage of a friend to protect another from harm.
3. Arnold Gragson's *The Underground Railroad*, is a narrative about helping a slave across a river to escape from slavery, illustrating courage to put one's life in danger for another person's freedom and dignity.

Analyzing actions. Students consider different scenarios in which the protagonist takes action. Then they decide whether the action is courageous, foolhardy, or for personal gain.

Level 2: Attention to Facts and Skills
Focus on detail and prototypical examples, Build knowledge

Community courage. Students gather stories of courage from community members. Community members are asked to discuss how they overcame their fear. They present these as dramas, poems, song, drawings, essays, and so on. Community members are invited to attend the presentations.

Practice being brave. Offer opportunities for students to be brave in the classroom (such as standing up for an unpopular child). Coach them on being brave. Note progress.

Starred ★ activities within each subskill go together!

EA-5 Cultivating Courage

Cultivating Courage
by Managing Fear
Ideas for Developing Skills

Assessment Hints

Manage Fear

Use multiple-choice, true-false, short answer, or essay tests to assess student knowledge about the characteristics of courageousness (vs. cowardice or foolhardiness).

Use a real-life biography of someone who overcame fear and have students describe the behaviors of the courageous person.

Have students write reports, based on their observations or interviews, of how overcame their fears to perform a courageous act; students can present their reports to the class.

Have students keep a journal of their experiences with overcoming fear; assess the journal entries.

Have students role play scenarios and demonstrate overcoming fear.

Starred ★ activities within each subskill go together!

Level 3: Practice Procedures
Set goals, Plan steps of problem solving, Practice skills

★ **Personal examples of daily courage.** Students share their efforts at following through on scary but important decisions.

Being courageous and reaching out. Discuss how to reach out to students who may be in need of friends. Have students practice and report.

Admitting mistakes. Discuss how admitting mistakes takes courage. Have students find examples of people admitting mistakes. Have students practice admitting mistakes in class and outside of class.

Manage emotionality. Emotionality (called neuroticism by some psychologists) is the tendency to succumb to mood swings, stress, passions, anxiety, and sensitivity. Focusing too much on negative emotions like fear, anxiety, sadness is related to several life-threatening diseases so for this and other reasons it is important to learn to counter your tendencies to dwell on negatives. Have students keep a daily journal recording the approximate percentage of time they spend thinking about negative things in contrast to thinking about positive things.

Cultivate serenity. Cianciosi (2001) suggests that meditation is a systematic, introspective practice to facilitate growth in three main areas: (1) Getting to know the mind by studying the inner world of mental and emotional states. (2) Training the mind by building awareness, concentration, and serenity. (3) Freeing the mind by gradually reducing the power of negative tendencies. The three go hand in hand. Mindfulness is the skill to be developed in meditation. During meditation one can try to empty the mind, focus on an image or sound. A Christian approach to meditation often focuses on the words or image of Jesus. All this is to happen gently over time. With practice, one develops serenity—the experience of rest, tranquility, even joy. Have students practice on a daily basis for several months.

Level 4: Integrate Knowledge and Procedures
Execute plans, Solve problems

★ **Mentoring others to overcome fears.** Have students work with a younger student to help them learn to overcome their fears about school. Students report back regularly.

Having a mentor. Have students work with high school students or adults on being courageous.

Cultivating Courage by Standing Up Under Pressure

Rachel Carson wrote the book *Silent Spring* in 1962 about how people are hurting the environment. At that time, no one was worried about the environment. Her work was initially dismissed. However, with persistence and courage, she stood by her findings. With time her work was recognized as valuable by the U.S. government.

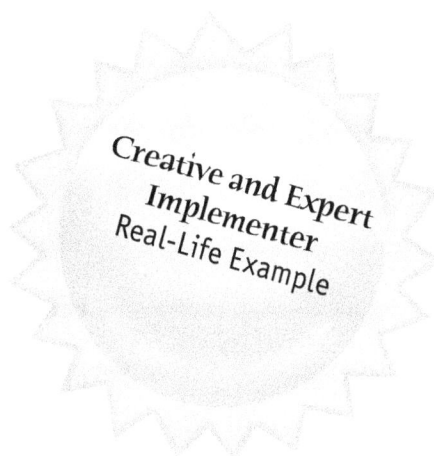

Ideas for Developing Skills

Level 1: Immersion in Examples and Opportunities
Attend to the big picture, Learn to recognize basic patterns

Out-group well being. Identify situations that are harmful to out-groups (groups the student is not a part of) and consider means to rectify the situation. Students identify a situation at school where some children are rejected. Brainstorm on how to change the situation.

Stories about courage. Have students find examples (e.g., from newspapers, stories) of people who were brave by taking an unpopular position. Read these examples and discuss.

Uniqueness. Discuss how individuals are different and the benefits of having differences. Where do people get messages that being different is not good? Where do people get messages (and what kind) about how they should look, act, think?

Level 2: Attention to Facts and Skills
Focus on detail and prototypical examples, Build knowledge

Supporting others. (1) The student identifies ways to support people who are not part of his/her groups. (2) The student describes three options for including a rejected student in a group.

Attending to pressures from the media. (1) Have students analyze the pressures the media puts on individuals in terms of how they should look or act to be successful. (2) Do a historical analysis of media images of women and men, boys and girls.

Starred ★ activities within each subskill go together!

Cultivating Courage
by Standing Up Under Pressure
Ideas for Developing Skills

Level 3: Practice Procedures
Set goals, Plan steps of problem solving, Practice skills

Peer well-being. The student describes optional actions for standing up for others. For example, he or she identifies three ways to stand up for a peer who doesn't speak English.

Avoiding drugs. Discuss how to avoid drug use by inviting a community member to talk about personal experiences with substance abuse, the consequences, and personal responsibility.

Avoiding violence. Use group discussions and role-plays to address how to say "no" to verbal and physical aggression.

Local examples of courage. Students choose someone from their chools (they do not have to name the individual) to write an essay about. Students write about something that the student did in or outside of class that demonstrated courage in the face of ridicule or disapproval. **Assess** for the elements of courageous behavior listed above.

Role play being courageous. Students act out situations that require courage, imitating situations they have read about.

Media pressure refusal.
Teacher should:
- Help student identify areas the media pressures them (look at television, magazines, billboards, music videos and songs, movies, video games, etc.).
- Define media pressure: the subtle messages that the media says about who you should be, how you should look, how you should act, what is beautiful, what is success, what you should focus your life on, what you should do with your time, what you should think of your peers, what you should think of adults, etc.
- Discuss typical portrayals that the media presents and why they might have so much power.
- Discuss what a thoughtful mentor would advise vs. what the media "advises."
- Discuss the consequences of accepting or not accepting media messages.
- Discuss "who do I want to give control to?"—media, myself, peers, tobacco companies, etc.
- Saying "no" to media images and messages can be hard so we need to practice different ways.

EA-5 Cultivating Courage

Starred activities within each subskill go together!

Cultivating Courage
by Standing Up Under Pressure
Ideas for Developing Skills

Level 3 (continued)

Students practice 3-step refusal process. (a) Check out the message and apply the self-esteem rule: Does it make you feel bad about yourself as you are now? (b) Decide whether or not you can put up with it without being influenced. (c) Act quickly to avoid being influenced, using one of these options: (1) change the channel, turn the page; (2) turn it off or throw it away or leave; (3) talk back to the image or message with a counter message; (4) make a joke about it; (5) suggest a better message; (6) write an email to complain about the message; (7) boycott the product; (8) start a petition against the product; (9) keep track of what messages and how many break the self-esteem rule. Think of other responses. **Assess** with a written test on identifying messages, or on the refusal approaches generally, or in response to particular scenarios.

Cultural differences in courage. Students talk to members of different cultures in the community. Students ask for stories of courage from the culture. These stories are gathered, written up by the students, and discussed in class.

Level 4: Integrate Knowledge and Procedures
Execute plans, Solve problems

Standing up to the media. After identifying offensive messages in the media, students create and take an action plan. They can begin by writing letters of complaint, and move to planning and carrying out a demonstration or boycott.

Testing standing up. Put together several examples of common situations in school where a person is pressured to do something they should not do or don't need to do. With the consent of the students, ask other teachers/ students to test them (as if real but not). Students should expect to be tested but should not know when, by whom or on what.

Starred ★ activities
within each subskill
go together!

Assessment Hints

Standing Up under Pressure

Use a real-life biography of someone who took an unpopular position and have students describe the characteristics and behaviors of the person·

Present a written scenario or video clip of a situation in which a character should take an unpopular position and have students respond in writing about what the character should do and how s/he should do it·

Have students write reports, based on observations or interviews, of how others took an unpopular position and demonstrated courage; students can present their reports to the class·

Have students role play scenarios and demonstrate courageous behaviors·

EA-5 Cultivating Courage

Cultivating Courage by Managing Change & Uncertainty

Jim Lovell (depicted by Tom Hanks in the movie *Apollo 13*) commanded the spaceship Apollo 13 that malfunctioned on its way to the moon for a landing. Lovell lost his dream of stepping on the moon because it was all they could do to get home safely, improvising as they went.

Ideas for Developing Skills

Level 1: Immersion in Examples and Opportunities
Attend to the big picture, Learn to recognize basic patterns

Catalysts for change. Discuss good reasons that people might change their minds about something (e.g., new information, new research findings, hard experience).

Historic changers. Present examples of beloved figures who demonstrated the ability to change their minds (e.g., Abraham Lincoln and the goals of the civil war, Anwar Sadat and Egypt's relation to Israel).

Things that change. Brainstorm about all the things that change in life. Sort by categories, which should include physical changes (like growing up, hormones), social changes (like relationships, members of class, members of community), government, rights and privileges (being able to drive), work, purchasing power, status, possessions, etc. Ask students to think about each of the categories (or subcategories) and how important it really is in helping them reach their goals. For the things that students mark as very important, have them think of alternative actions or goals. For example, I want to get a scholarship to college. If I don't, I could get loans, borrow money from a relative, or work to put myself through school.

What changes in a person? Brainstorm about what changes in an individual (e.g., needs, beliefs, priorities, knowledge, information/facts) and discuss what the students have to anticipate.

Level 2: Attention to Facts and Skills
Focus on detail and prototypical examples, Build knowledge

Negative reactions to change. Hate groups organize around deep fears of change. See www.tolerance.org for downloadable materials on how to confront hate at school, hate in the community and for more information about hate groups.

Cultivating Courage
by Managing Change & Uncertainty
Ideas for Developing Skills

Level 2 (continued)

Role models' reaction to change. Study role models who have faced catastrophic change and examine how they faced it. For example, actor Christopher Reeve who became a quadriplegic after an equestrian accident; Lou Gehrig, late baseball player, and Stephen Hawking, physicist, who both were diagnosed with ALS (Amyotrophic Lateral Sclerosis); and Thomas Edison who became increasingly deaf after age 12 when someone picked him up by his ears.

Competition. Ask business leaders to speak about how they deal with competition in products and ideas, and how they take advantage of change in the marketplace.

Information. (1) Libraries. Ask the local librarian to discuss how the library deals with the vast changes in the type, access and amount of information. (2) Civil service. Ask a civil servant who works in a quickly changing area (pollution control, environment, forestry, energy, security) and ask how they access the latest information and how they make use of it.

Social service. Invite social service workers to discuss changes in population, diversity, and needs in the populace and how their work manages it all.

Level 3: Practice Procedures
Set goals, Plan steps of problem solving, Practice skills

Changes in a domain. Invite speakers from domains where conditions change and workers must adjust their goals and reactions. What kind of changes do they face? Have them describe how they are flexible and have multiple skills for dealing with change.

What is uncertain in a domain? Understanding uncertainty means realizing that humans are limited in what they can know by their machinery, that humans have access to only part of reality, and that the future cannot be fully known in advance (Baltes & Straudinger, 2000). Investigate what aspects of a particular domain are still uncertain.

Survey of managing change. Have students gather all the information they can find about how people manage change and compile it into one large list.

Cultivate self reliance. Investigate the nature of self reliance? What do self reliant people look like? Classic works to study include writings by Emerson and Thoreau. Current work includes those who support sustainable or simple living.

Cultivating Courage
by Managing Change & Uncertainty
Ideas for Developing Skills

Level 3 (continued)

Setback or challenge? Look at what famous people say about their set-backs—what language do they use? How do they respond? Do they give up?

Level 4: Integrate Knowledge and Procedures
Execute plans, Solve problems

Global climate change. Investigate what is contributing to global warming in your community. Then make an action plan to help the community cut back on the cause. Use the steps suggested by Lewis' (1998) *Kid's Guide to Social Action* (written for kids to use with worksheets and concrete guidelines): (1) Choose a problem in the neighborhood (Does an area feel unsafe? Smell bad? Look terrible? Are there needy people?). (2) Do your research (How do community members feel about the problem? What is the history of the problem?). (3) Brainstorm possible solutions and choose the one that seems most possible and will make the most difference. (4) Build coalitions of support. Find all the people that agree with you (neighborhood, community, city, state, businesses, agencies). (5) Figure out (with the help of your coalition) who is your opposition and work with them on overcoming their objections. (6) Advertise (send out a news release, call tv, radio, newspaper reporters, churches). (7) Raise money if you need to. (8) Carry out your solution. Make a list of the steps you need to take (e.g., write letters, give speeches, pass petitions). (9) Evaluate and reflect on whether the plan is working. Did you try everything, should you change something? Celebrate what you have done by writing about it, dramatizing it, drawing it. (10) Don't give up. Find the thing that will work.

Assessment Hints

Manage change and uncertainty

Use reflective activities such as essays, journaling, keeping a report diary.

Use creative activities such as poems, songs, music, plays, visual art.

Create a Climate
to Cultivate Courage

Assign responsibility for others.

Point out people who have taken risks in their field of study and how it helped a group of people.

Teach them concern for social justice and citizen action.

Foster these attitudes:
   Courage is important.
   Risk-taking is not necessarily courage.
   You can learn to be courageous.
   Stand up for what you believe.
   Admit one's own mistakes.
   Refrain from doing what everyone else does when it is wrong.
   Do the right thing, not the easy thing.
   Confront others when they hurt someone.
   Ask for help when it is needed.
   Do not give up when things go wrong.
   Do things even if you might fail.
   Put self at risk for a good cause.
   Overcome fear.

Sample Student Self-Monitoring
Cultivating Courage

Encourage active learning by having students learn to monitor their own learning

Manage fear
I am not afraid to try something new.
I never admit mistakes. (NOT)
I give up when things go wrong. (NOT)

Stand up under pressure
I confront others when they hurt someone.
I say no to drinking, smoking, and using drugs.
I stand up for what I believe, even when others are against it.
If others do the wrong thing, I do not do it just to be one of
   them.
I confront others when they hurt someone.

Manage change and uncertainty
I know the kinds of changes that occur in people's lives.
I can anticipate changes in my life.
I know how to react positively to change.

Persevering

(Develop Perseverance)

WHAT
Perseverance enables individuals to complete actions that are important to them and others. Without it, many ethical actions would fail at
the sight of the first obstacle or difficulty. Perseverance involves skills
of steadfastness, resourcefulness and other competencies related to
successful completion of goals.

WHY
Perseverance is important for the completion of an ethical action.
Children can be successfully instructed to talk to themselves about
not doing something, and instructed on how to distract themselves
from unwanted behavior. A form of self-talk to complete a task can be
a useful technique to help one find the ego strength to complete an
ethical action—at any age.

EA-6 Persevering

SUBSKILLS OVERVIEW
    Be steadfast
    Overcome obstacles
    Build competence

Web Wise
Find multiple lesson plans with assessments for building character at www.goodcharacter.com

Persevering
by Being Steadfast

Oprah Winfrey persevered until she built a successful career and found a lifestyle that helped her keep fit and happy. Abused as a child, she overcame many obstacles and frustrations to succeed in school. She has also exhibited excellent self-control skills in (1) building her career from a journalist to a well-known and loved talk show host, and (2) successfully managing her health through a balanced diet and routine exercise.

Ideas for Developing Skills

Level 1: Immersion in Examples and Opportunities
Attend to the big picture, Learn to recognize basic patterns

Delaying gratification. Delayed gratification (rather than instant gratification) is a vital skill necessary for meeting goals. This includes enduring frustration, resisting temptation, and distraction. (1) Discuss characters in stories and films that demonstrate this skill (or don't). (2) Discuss examples in a particular subject area (e.g., necessary for success in the field).

Impulse control. Observe how people control their emotions (e.g., anger) in order to get along better with others, or to reach their goals. (1) Use stories or videos. (2) Use examples from the particular subject area.

Being steadfast and loyal. Students read stories about loyalty then discuss the focus it requires.

Staying single-minded. Read about the importance of single-mindedness in accomplishing a difficult task.

Level 2: Attention to Facts and Skills
Focus on detail and prototypical examples, Build knowledge

Examples of delayed gratification. Students conduct interviews and ask for examples of delayed gratification in their lives. What techniques did the interviewees use? (1) Interview elders from the community about general experiences. (2) Interview adults from particular fields of work/study.

Starred activities within each subskill go together!

Persevering
by Being Steadfast
Ideas for Developing Skills

Level 2 (continued)

Persistence at school. (1) Discuss the elements of persistence. For example, here are elements from Lufi and Cohen's (1987) Persistence Scale for Children: completing tasks, keep trying to solve a problem if it's hard, completing tasks without encouragement, asking for an explanation if it is difficult to understand something, getting help from an adult instead of working on one's own. Students work in groups of 3-4 to identify elements of persistent behavior that is helpful in school and learning. (2) Have students interview older students about these techniques. (3) Have students interview college graduates and people with graduate degrees in particular fields of study.

Finding out about steadfastness. Students interview community members about their experiences with loyalty and what it takes.

Finding out about thoroughness. Students interview community members in an area of interest about how they are thorough in their work and what happens if they are not.

Finding out about standards. Students interview community members about what kinds of standards they have for themselves and how they developed them.

Finding out about avoiding distractions. Students interview community members about what they do to counter or avoid distractions from their work.

Level 3: Practice Procedures
Set goals, Plan steps of problem solving, Practice skills

Role play delaying gratification. Students act out scenarios where they delay gratification. (1) Interpersonal self-control such as waiting to tell a secret. (2) Health and decision making such as waiting until of age to try alcohol.

Practicing impulse control. (1) Learn techniques for controlling anger and frustration: Breathing deeply, counting backward, deep breathing, thinking about pleasant or peaceful imagery. (2) Control desire for candy or junk food: Eat a healthy food first and drink a glass of water. Take only a small portion of the junk food. (3) Practice some of the techniques used by the college students and experts (interviewed in Level 2).

Starred ★ activities
within each subskill
go together!

Persevering
by Being Steadfast
Ideas for Developing Skills

Level 3 (continued)

Practicing steadfastness all together. Is the student able to stay focused on a task, ignoring distractions, until the job is done? In small groups or large group, have students make a list of techniques learned from the interviews that they will practice. Have them select the techniques they will practice first and make a plan when and how to do so. Daily or weekly, have the group discuss progress on learning the techniques. When they have questions, have them communicate with the community mentors for more guidance.

Practicing thoroughness individually. Is the student aware of high standards, able to carry them out, and motivated to complete a task in an excellent way? With information from their interviews above, have students apply what they learned to their own work. Have them journal about the experience and share it with the community member they interviewed previously. Have the community member give a report on how the student is doing.

Level 4: Integrate Knowledge and Procedures
Execute plans, Solve problems

Integrating delayed gratification. (1) Students select a reward that they will withhold from themselves for a period of time (e.g., soft drinks for a week) until they complete, for example, a difficult assignment. (2) Students coach younger students in a particular task.

Integrating impulse control. Students put themselves in slightly tempting situations and flex their impulse control skills. For example, a student could set a bag of candy in his or her room but not take any.

Mentoring steadfastness. Have students mentor younger students on what they have learned from the community member's coaching them previously.

Starred ★ activities
within each subskill
go together!

Persevering
by Being Steadfast
Ideas for Developing Skills

Level 4 (continued)

Mentoring thoroughness. Have students mentor younger students on what they have learned from the community member's coaching them previously.

Assessment Hints

Be Steadfast

Use multiple-choice, true-false, short answer, or essay tests to assess student knowledge of self-control strategies.

Use a new conflict (written or video clip) and have students respond in writing about what delayed gratification or impulse control strategies they would use.

Have students write reports, based on observations or interviews, of what they learned about delayed gratification and impulse control, being steadfast, and avoiding distractions. Students can present their reports to class.

Have students role play delayed gratification and impulse control scenarios and demonstrate self-control skills.

Have students keep a journal of their own experiences with thoroughness, setting standards, being steadfast, and avoiding distractions; assess the journal entries.

Persevering
by Overcoming Obstacles

Creative and Expert Implementer Real-Life Example

Former President **Richard Nixon** overcame many obstacles in order to become President of the United States. He first ran for President against John F. Kennedy in 1960, in which he lost. In 1962, he ran for governor of California and lost. In 1968, Nixon ran for President again and won this time, becoming the 37th President of the United States.

Ideas for Developing Skills

Level 1: Immersion in Examples and Opportunities
Attend to the big picture, Learn to recognize basic patterns

Creative alternatives for overcoming obstacles. Focus on people who figured a way out of a predicament. Discuss how people invent subroutines to work around an obstacle. (1) Read stories (e.g., Odysseus and the Cyclops). (2) Discuss the choices people have in a particular subject area.

Role models of perseverance. Identify different people who have persevered for others: (1) Students read stories/watch films about people who did not give up in trying to help others, discussing what they did to keep on task. (2) Discuss role models from particular fields.

Level 2: Attention to Facts and Skills
Focus on detail and prototypical examples, Build knowledge

Read stories and write essays about overcoming obstacles. Students read books on historical and fictional people who displayed persistent behavior to overcome obstacles to meet their goals. Students write essays on the characteristics of the people who were persistent. Examples:
1. Students read the autobiography, *Narrative of the Life of Frederick Douglass*, the story of Frederick Douglass' escape from slavery.
2. Students read a biography of Leonardo da Vinci, who conducted scientific research opposed by the Catholic Church.
3. Students read *The Joy Luck Club* by Amy Tan (1989), in which four women escape oppressive relationships and immigrate to America.
4. Select writings about members of a particular profession or field.

Starred activities within each subskill go together!

Persevering
by Overcoming Obstacles
Ideas for Developing Skills

Level 2 (continued)

Examples of facing obstacles. Discuss the different obstacles there might be when striving for a particular goal in a particular area of life. For example, in discussing human rights, address the obstacles Martin Luther King, Jr. faced when trying to gain equal rights for U.S. blacks: what did he/could he do to overcome them? Invent ways he could have gotten around the obstacles.

Level 3: Practice Procedures
Set goals, Plan steps of problem solving, Practice skills

Procedures for overcoming obstacles in a particular field or subject matter. Discuss systematic ways to overcome an obstacle. For example: (a) Think of other ways to complete the task. (b) Rank the options for feasibility and try each one in order. (c) Ask someone for ideas or do research on the task. (d) Ask a skilled person to help you complete the task.

Level 4: Integrate Knowledge and Procedures
Execute plans, Solve problems

Challenging boredom. In their journals, students describe their techniques for overcoming fatigue and boredom when carrying out a responsibility (e.g., caring for a 'baby' (e.g., a diapered sack of flour over a week's time or caring for current toys that demand constant attention or they 'die'). This can be applied to particular assignments in particular subject areas.

Obstacles in my life. Ask students to identify the two most important goals they have for their lives. Ask them to identify what needs to happen first to help them reach their goals, what obstacles might prevent them from taking the first steps, and what can they do to overcome the obstacles. (If an obstacle is something they cannot change like their size, they should find another goal.) Once they have this figured out, ask them to begin to take the first steps towards at least one of their goals. Have them record their progress and report periodically.

Starred ★ activities
within each subskill
go together!

Assessment Hints

Overcome Obstacles

Use multiple-choice, true-false, short answer, or essay tests to assess student knowledge about different strategies or behaviors that one can use to overcome obstacles.

Use a real-life biography of someone who overcame many obstacles (written or video clip) and have students describe the characteristics and behaviors of the person that helped him/her overcome the obstacles.

Have students role play scenarios and demonstrate behaviors of overcoming obstacles.

Persevering
by Building Competence

Creative and Expert Implementer Real-Life Example

Christopher Reeve (who played Superman in the movies) had an equestrian accident that left him a quadriplegic. He could have given up in life and stayed home quietly. Instead, he became a spokesman for those with spinal injuries, traveling to speak about the importance of research in spinal injuries.

Ideas for Developing Skills

Level 1: Immersion in Examples and Opportunities
Attend to the big picture, Learn to recognize basic patterns

Study self-efficacy. Discuss how, for a particular field, small successes give a person confidence to keep trying and try harder things. Find examples in literature, television and movies, or in a particular subject area.

What is competency?
(1) What are you good at? Have students interview adults in the community about what they feel they are good at doing. How do they know they are good at something?
(2) Discuss what it means for a person to be good at something. (a) What kinds of things are people good at? Identify examples of people who are good at each thing the class comes up with. (b) What are the similarities among these people who are very competent? What are the differences? (c) How did they get to be competent? What did all of them do? What was different about what they did to reach competence?
(3) Select a domain or field of study. Invite speakers from that domain to discuss the nature of competence in the domain and how to reach it.

Who has the competency I'd like to have? Have students write down three skills they would like to have. For each skill, identify a person who has perfected the skill. Have students study and write about one of these people to find out how they reached their level of performance.

Persevering
by Building Competence
Ideas for Developing Skills

Level 1 (continued)

Competence is a resiliency factor.

(1) Discuss with students the importance of developing competence. The students who have the most troubled backgrounds may benefit the most from competency development. Yet virtually everyone will face a high-risk time in their lives (e.g., a time when stresses are very high and temptations to use drugs or take criminal action will be available) and so everyone should make sure they have the skills that may protect them. A particular skill that is shared with others is a protective factor against high-risk environments (for example, playing piano at church, playing on the basketball team, caring for younger siblings). Discuss the particular skills students have to share and how to develop weak or new skills. Set up a plan for developing a particular shareable skill with each student.

(2) There are several types of general competencies that are protective against risk factors such as parental neglect or abuse, poverty, negative role models, and so on. These general skills include (Benard, 1995): (a) Social skills (e.g., the ability to elicit positive responses from others and being responsive to them, being flexible and able to move between cultures, showing empathy and a sense of humor). (b) Problem-solving skills (e.g., resourceful in seeking help from others, planning skills, thinking creatively, critically and reflectively). (c) Autonomy skills (e.g., having a sense of identity—including resisting negative messages about oneself from others, an ability to act independently, a sense of task mastery, the ability to exert a little control over one's environment, including distancing oneself from a dysfunctional situation). (d) Critical consciousness (awareness of the structures that oppress one—like a drug-addicted parent, dangerous home neighborhood, racist society—and having strategies to overcome the oppression). (e) Sense of purpose (e.g., positive life goals and educational aspirations, hopeful and optimistic attitudes, a sense of spiritual connection, and persistence). Discuss each of these with students and how to develop the skills in the classroom and school. Have students take charge of their own development through planning and carrying out little steps towards development.

Level 2: Attention to Facts and Skills
Focus on detail and prototypical examples, Build knowledge

Self-talk. Find examples of and discuss how to 'cheerlead' for yourself in different situations. What behaviors help you do your best and reach excellence? (1) Students discuss self-talk and behaviors that help one persevere. (2) Students interview older students or adults about general behaviors. (3) Students interview adults in roles they admire or strive for in a particular field.

Persevering
by Building Competence
Ideas for Developing Skills

Level 2 (continued)

What are my competencies? Have students mark what they are good at, what other people think they are good at, and what they are not good at but would like to be. Use categories like the following: School subjects (i.e., math, science, etc.), Social arena (e.g., making friends, being a group member, having a support group, dealing with bullying), Physical (i.e., sport, dance, etc.), Intrapersonal (i.e., self-reflection, knowing my feelings), Artistic, Creative and Inventive, Leadership, Critical thinking, and so on.

How do people build competency? Have students select a person they admire doing something they would like to do some day (work of some sort). Students investigate the regimen of study the person used and uses. Students model a plan of study for themselves based on what they learn.

How do people build competency in particular areas? Have students study successful people in a particular domain (e.g., research, actuarial science, art, etc.). They should find out what a typical day is like for the person now and what kind of effort it took on a daily basis to get to where they are.

Level 3: Practice Procedures
Set goals, Plan steps of problem solving, Practice skills

Examples of pushing oneself in helping others. Students interview elders about their personal experiences of (1) how they persevered in trying to help others; (2) how they persevered in working towards a goal that helped humanity.

Self-help. Have students practice ways to coach oneself to reach excellence in skills like these for a particular subject area: (1) Persistence in mental and physical tasks; (2) Keep trying to solve a problem if it's hard; (3) Completing tasks without encouragement from others.

Building a competency. Have students identify a competency they would like to build or improve upon. Set up a mentor or a coach if they don't have one (this could be an older student or neighbor). Have them practice for a period of months, reporting their progress as they go.

Persevering
by Building Competence
Ideas for Developing Skills
Level 4: Integrate Knowledge and Procedures
Execute plans, Solve problems

Daily persevering. Every day for a week give each student a difficult problem to solve (e.g., students try solving a Rubik's Cube on their own). Time how long each student stays on task without giving up. Then discuss what they could have done differently. As each day progresses, students should improve. The following week, have the students choose a skill they want to improve and follow the same procedures: time themselves on task each day, trying longer each time. Students report on their progress.

Mentoring. Have students work with a mentor or mentor a younger student in self-coaching for a difficult task. This can be across subjects or for particular subjects.

Share a competency. Students work on presenting a competency that they can share with younger students or community members. This could be a musical program, a play, artwork, special knowledge (e.g., gardening in pots), and so on. Those without individual skill can work with others. Once they have worked up a specific performance or product, schedule a performance, a showing, or a teach in.

Assessment Hints

Build competence

Use multiple-choice, true-false, short answer, or essay tests to assess student knowledge of strategies to push oneself.

Have students write reports, based on observations or interviews, of what they learned about pushing oneself.

Have students role play perseverance scenarios and demonstrate skills in pushing oneself.

Create a Climate
to Persevere

Regularly discuss the importance of finishing a task, as a group or individual.

Regularly point out what would happen if people did not persevere until a job was done (e.g., the highway, a bridge, your house, your car) and how it would affect people around them.

Discuss the importance of persevering in meeting your responsibilities to others.

Selections to Post in the Classroom
for Persevering

What you need to know for success in school
(Adapted from Marzano, 2003; Paul, 1987)

1. Attitudes affect behavior
2. What you believe/think about affects your behavior
3. You have some control over your attitudes
4. Learning anything requires commitment (decision to put your energies into a task)
5. General attitudes to foster: effort pays off; I can perform the task
6. You can learn from failure
7. Push yourself
8. You can monitor and control your commitment, attitudes, and attention

Sample Student Self-Monitoring
Persevering
Encourage active learning by having students learn to monitor their own learning

Be steadfast
I wait to reward myself until I've finished my work.
I don't wait until the last minute to do my work.
I lose control when I am angry. (NOT)
I control my feelings of anger.
I resist my impulses to disobey rules.
I do what I want, even if it hurts others. (NOT)
I resist peer pressure to do things that are hurtful.
I complete my assigned chores.
I work hard in class.
I finish my homework.
I complete the assigned work in class.
I follow the rules.
I know what my temptations (to stop working) are.
I avoid temptation.
I know how to motivate myself when I get tired.
I know how to 'unbore' myself when I am working.
I can help others 'unbore' themselves while we continue working.
   What is good about 'unboring' myself is staying focused and
      committed to finishing.

Overcome obstacles
I know techniques to use to encourage myself when things get
   hard.
I don't take on more things than I can handle.
I break things into little steps to complete a task little by little.

Build competence
I keep trying until I solve a problem.
Even when things get hard, I keep working.
If I decide not to do something, I don't give in.

Ethical Action 7

Working Hard

(Work Hard)

WHAT

Hard work means spending a great deal of energy, time and 'sweat' to accomplish a worthwhile task. It means continuing toward a goal even when the goal is far off and the journey gets boring or tedious. In order to work had successfully, one must have skills of setting reachable goals, managing time and taking charge of one's life.

WHY

Related to social and economic success in societies all around the world (Sowell, 1994, 1996), hard work for future gain is a necessary skill among citizens for an economically successful society. Hard work is considered an important component of one's character and should be encouraged in all students.

SUBSKILLS OVERVIEW

Set reachable goals
Manage time
Take charge of your life

Web Wise
Have students test their locus of control at http://discoveryhealth.queendom.com
Use material from the website:
   http://www.bygpub.com/books/tg2rw/excerpts.htm, especially Chapters 0 and 7 for jigsaw
   material (see Appendix for jigsaw guidelines).
www.healthfinder.gov

Working Hard by Setting Reachable Goals

Dave Thomas, founder of Wendy's restaurant, had a child-hood dream of owning his own restaurant. He opened his first Wendy's in Columbus, Ohio in 1969, and set reachable goals for the next 30 years to have his restaurants enjoyed by millions of people in the U.S., Canada, and several other countries.

Creative and Expert Implementer Real-Life Example

Ideas for Developing Skills

Level 1: Immersion in Examples and Opportunities
Attend to the big picture, Learn to recognize basic patterns

Breaking tasks into subgoals. Discuss the need to break tasks into subtasks. Use an example like following a recipe. Find examples in stories and videos. Give students simple tasks to break into sub-tasks.

Story examples of setting subgoals. In the stories read above, identify the subgoals that were (or may have been) set by the workers.

Level 2: Attention to Facts and Skills
Focus on detail and prototypical examples, Build knowledge

Setting goals for a project. (1) Generate several (imaginary) goals and have students practice setting up the steps needed to reach the goals. (2) For an individual project, have students make a list of necessary subgoals or steps with a timeline to reach the final goal. Have them keep track of their progress using the list. Do they need to add or change a step? Does the goal need to be revised? Is the timeline realistic or does it need to be modified?

Setting classroom goals. Students work in groups of 3-4 to develop overall goals for the class. They should discuss how each goal affects learning. Short example: Students should include, among other things they decide are important:

   How often should each person report on current events to the class?
   How many books should they read as a class per year?
   How many written assignments should the class have per year?

Starred ★ activities within each subskill go together!

Working Hard
by Setting Reachable Goals
Ideas for Developing Skills

Level 3: Practice Procedures
Set goals, Plan steps of problem solving, Practice skills

Goals in learning using practice and drill. Have students identify an area of academic weakness and make a strategic plan with step-by-step goals to reach a particular level of improvement. They record their progress day by day and summarize it in weekly reports.

Level 4: Integrate Knowledge and Procedures
Execute plans, Solve problems

Select a challenging project. Have students take on a difficult project and complete it using the skills of setting goals, practice and drill. For example, a student could organize a petition drive to rid the cafeteria of Styrofoam cups.

Setting reachable goals. Ask parents/guardians to help the student select some school or personal goal(s) to aim for over the period of a month or two. Have the student turn in a paper listing what the goals are with their signature. After the set period of time, pull out the sheet and ask the student and parent/guardian to confer on progress with you.

Assess whether or not the goal is realistic (Borba, 1999). Have students set a goal and then work with a partner to answer the following questions to gauge how realistic the goal is. (1) Can you picture exactly what you want to accomplish? (2) Do you want to take responsibility for achieving this? (3) Have you thought through all the steps necessary to reach your goal? (4) Can you explain the specifics of your plan to someone else? (5) Does it make sense for you to do this? (6) Do you have the skills to achieve your goal? (7) Do you have the necessary support to succeed? (8) Do you have enough time to accomplish your goal?

Assessment Hints

Set Reachable Goals

Present a written scenario or video clip of a task and have students respond in writing about how to break the task into sub-goals.

Have students keep a journal of their own experiences in setting goals and reflecting how successful their goal-setting was; assess the journal entries.

Starred activities within each subskill go together!

Working Hard by Managing Time

Thomas Edison was known for how he managed his time throughout his life. As a working adolescent, he spent his lunch hours reading books to further his education. As an inventor, he would try hundreds if not thousands of materials to use, for example, in making a lightbulb or a storage battery.

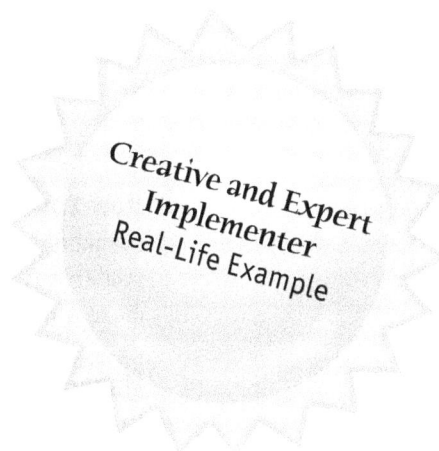

Creative and Expert Implementer Real-Life Example

Ideas for Developing Skills

Level 1: Immersion in Examples and Opportunities
Attend to the big picture, Learn to recognize basic patterns

Effective students. Bring in successful students to discuss how they manage their time. What are their priorities when they study? How do they set their goals for the week, day or hour? How do they know how much time something will take? How do they stay on schedule? What do they do if they get off schedule? What if something unexpected happens? Ask them for tips for students to use.

Sport heroes. Bring in a sport hero or other celebrity. Ask them to discuss their time management. How do they set their goals for the week, day or hour? How do they know how much time something will take? How do they stay on schedule? Ask them to give any suggestions they might have.

Self-employed. Bring in several self-employed business people to discuss the nature of their lives. How much time do they put into the business and how do they schedule it? How do they set their goals for the week, day or hour? How do they know how much time something will take? How do they stay on schedule?

Artists and writers. Invite local artists and writers to speak about their use of time. Ask them to discuss how they manage their creative energy as well. Do they set specific goals for the week, day or hour?

Level 2: Attention to Facts and Skills
Focus on detail and prototypical examples, Build knowledge

Elements of time management. Students role play time management as a student, a parent, a teacher, and as if they had the career they most admire: (a) Make a list of the most important things you want to do at the beginning of the day. (b) Number them in order of importance. (c) Start at the beginning. (d) Recheck your priorities throughout the time period.

Working Hard
by Managing Time
Ideas for Developing Skills

Level 2 (continued)

How time management varies across domains. After bringing in speakers from a variety of careers to talk about time management, have students fill in the blanks finding out information about other careers. Then make a master chart of the differences among the careers.

Managing environmental time. The environment is warming a thousand times faster than it ever has, due to human activity. Discuss the evidence and the consequences for global warming. Discuss how time plays a role here. Who benefits from delaying action? Who is most harmed?

Remedying unjust serving of time. Discuss how convictions to prison and even to death row can be misguided in this and other countries. Amnesty International has many examples. Bob Herbert described the injustice carried out in Tulia, Texas, in 2002. Who benefits from delaying changing the system that brings about the injustice? Who is most harmed?

Time commitments. (1) Have students take stock of what they spend their time doing. Have them write down their exact schedule for a day, indicating how many minutes were spent doing each activity. (2) Then have students reflect on the following questions, one at a time. What are my commitments? What captures my heart and attention most? What are my responsibilities? How much time do they require? Am I spending my time according to what makes me feel centered and fulfilled, or do I need to reprioritize my time allotments? (3) Ask students to make a plan for change.

Level 3: Practice Procedures
Set goals, Plan steps of problem solving, Practice skills

Paired school work management. Have students work in pairs on a time management plan for class or a special project.

Practicing time management. Students practice time management each day for a week or more for their time (1) at school and (2) at home during the week and (3) at home on the weekend. (a) Make a list of the most important things you want to do at the beginning of the day. (b) Number them in order of importance. (c) Start at the beginning. (d) Recheck your priorities throughout the time period.

Working Hard
by Managing Time
Ideas for Developing Skills

Level 4: Integrate Knowledge and Procedures
Execute plans, Solve problems

Accomplishment outside of school. Work with an adult, a mentor or experienced student on time management for accomplishing something outside of school (e.g., artistic project, your own business, environmental clean up). Completion of the project is the assessment.

Group time management. A group of students working on a project together should create a time management plan and then carry it out.

Planning for college or a career. Have students make a master plan for post high school, up to age 25. They identify the goals they have and how they can start taking steps now.

Assessment Hints

Manage time

Role play time management

Keeping a report diary

Actual demonstration of time management

GENERAL SELF-MONITORING
(Zimmerman, Bonner, & Kovach, 2002)

1. **Set goals**
2. **Know strategies for accomplishing goals**
3. **Use imagery**
   Imagine accomplishing the goal
   Imagine consequences of failure
4. **Self-instruction**
   Rehearse steps
   Cheer self on
   Prompt self
5. **Manage the time**
   Schedule the work to be done
6. **Self-monitoring**
   Keep records of accomplishments
7. **Self-evaluation**
   Avoid self-evaluation during brainstorming or creative work
   Use self-evaluation after completing components of strategies
8. **Self-consequences**
   Set high but reachable goals and work until they are reached
   Reward self AFTER task is completed
9. **Environmental Structuring**
   Select environment conducive to getting the work done
10. **Help Seeking**
    Get coaching from skilled person
    Get feedback from colleagues

Working Hard by Taking Charge of Your Life

Creative and Expert Implementer Real-Life Example

Venus and Serena Williams have worked very hard to achieve excellence in their tennis careers. The sisters have achieved excellence working both individually and as a team. Each sister playing individually has won several international tennis titles. Playing together in doubles tournaments, they have won numerous titles, including a gold medal at the 2000 Summer Olympics.

Ideas for Developing Skills

Level 1: Immersion in Examples and Opportunities
Attend to the big picture, Learn to recognize basic patterns

Areas for personal excellence. Discuss ways that individuals can be excellent (e.g., in mind, academics, relationships, values, self-attitudes, self-command, helpfulness). (1) Have each student identify what areas of excellence he or she would like to pursue by drawing/writing about his or her ideal self. Students create a goal sheet based on these ideals. (2) Have students focus on excellence as they participate in community service. Work or play? Students discuss what activities are work or play. Help them discriminate between situations that require much work and little work. Discuss how expertise development requires many hours of practice (which is often not 'fun').

Gathering stories about hard work. The students gather stories of the benefits of hard work from the community. The interviews focus on the subskills: working for excellence, being steadfast, thorough, setting reachable goals. The stories are compiled and displayed in story and picture (or photo) form (e.g., the bridge that was built, the people that were saved). Students can give oral presentations for the class, parents, and community members.

Perceptions of hard work. Students read stories about work and hen discuss how the characters were hard workers. The discussion could involve talking about (1) Hard work as a code: when does it apply? Do hard workers work hard all the time at all things? (2) The characters' perspectives about work: What did they think was work and what wasn't work? **Assess** with a report. (3) Students could also write a revision of the story where the characters are better workers than in the original story, possibly emphasizing the characters' attitudes toward work if applicable. **Assess** the revision.

Starred ★ activities within each subskill go together!

Examples of wisdom. Students research their cultural tradition for stories about wisdom and read/tell them in class.

Working Hard
by Taking Charge of Your Life
Ideas for Developing Skills

Level 1 (continued)

Who is school for? Who is in charge of my education? Help students take charge of their own education. Set short-term (e.g., to take an advanced math class next year) and long-term goals (e.g., to go to the local community college after high school). Ask a question in every class. Do homework. Try to get good grades. Hang around people who study and want to get good grades. The Search Institute's 40 assets include achievement motivation, good school performance, doing homework, and have high education aspirations (e.g., finish high school, go to college).

Level 2: Attention to Facts and Skills
Focus on detail and prototypical examples, Build knowledge

Skills of personal excellence. (1) Excellence in knowledge. What is most worth knowing? How does one decide? Have students interview experts in a field that interests them asking this and similar questions. Students report on the expert views. (2) Excellence in goals. What is most worth striving for? Have students interview people they think have reached excellent goals asking this and similar questions. Students report on the interviews. (3) Excellence in relationships. What does excellence mean for relationships? Have students interview elders they think have excellent relationships asking this and similar questions. Students report on the interviews.

Hard work in different cultural contexts. The students gather stories of the benefits of hard work from the different cultural groups in the community. These are compiled and displayed in story and picture (or photo) form (e.g., the bridge that was built, the people that were saved). Students can give oral presentations for the class, parents, and community members.

Identify different ways that wisdom is demonstrated. Students point out the differences in their collected stories of wisdom.

Locus of control. Locus of control refers to the degree to which people believe that an area in life is controlled by external factors or by internal factors. Those with internal locus of control are more effective at influencing their environment, more successful and more motivated to keep trying to solve problems and overcome obstacles. Have students test their locus of control at http://discoveryhealth.queendom.com

Taking charge of your future jigsaw activity. Use material from the website: http://www.bygpub.com/books/tg2rw/excerpts.htm, especially Chapters 0 and 7 for jigsaw material (see Appendix for jigsaw guidelines).

Starred ★ activities within each subskill go together!

Working Hard
by Taking Charge of Your Life
Ideas for Developing Skills

Level 3: Practice Procedures
Set goals, Plan steps of problem solving, Practice skills

Practicing personal excellence. Students identify an area in which they want to be excellent. It should be an area that harms no one. If not done in Level 3, have students interview persons they think exhibit this excellence and find out what goals they had, what skills they developed to reach their goals. Then students develop a short list of skills they will develop.

Practicing hard work. Students (with parents and teacher) identify a skill to be developed. Design a practice plan. With adult guidance they rehearse the skill until it is perfected.

Demonstrate wisdom in making decisions. Students role play situations like those in the traditional stories they collected.

Your life manager (adapted from McGraw, 2000). Ask students to think of themselves as their own life managers and respond to the following questions, designing a plan to make changes in the areas that are unsatisfactory: (a) Is your life manager making informed decisions? (b) Is your life manager taking care of you on all fronts—mentally, emotionally, spiritually and physically? (c) Is your life manager selecting relationships that are good for you? (d) Is your life manager giving you experiences that make you feel worthwhile? (e) Is your life manager making sure you see a purpose for your life? (f) Is your life manager giving you opportunities to build resilience?

Prevent burnout (some ideas from www.lifesplaybook.com). Help students take the following steps over the course of a week or month. (1) Keep track of what stresses you, when and how it happens. You can do this in a diary, emails to a friend, or just making a list. (2) Develop at least two or three ways to relax yourself when stress is triggered. For example, take a deep breath; close your eyes and imagine yourself relaxing on a beach, telling yourself "It doesn't bother me. It's no big deal." (3) Make a habit of breathing deeply everyday for a few minutes. (4) Several times a day, pay attention to any anxiety or tension you feel in your body. Scan your body head to toe to do this. When you find a tense spot, breathe deeply and think of relaxing it. (5) Establish a time and place that you relax for a few minutes a day. (6) During relaxation time, let go of fear, anger, resentment. Gradually, learn to do this all of the time.

Use exercise to enhance performance. Preliminary evidence suggests that physically active people have lower rates of anxiety and depression than people who get little exercise.

Starred activities within each subskill go together!

Working Hard
by Taking Charge of Your Life
Ideas for Developing Skills

Level 3 (continued)

Rejuvenate yourself. Help students make a habit of doing at least one of these things every week: (a) Turn off the television and spend time outside. (b) Read a magazine or book for fun. (c) Spend time conversing with family. (d) Enjoy relaxing music. (e) Volunteer to help a needy cause. (f) Create something like a drawing, poem, song, dance, invention, game, meal. (g) Create something for someone else like a thank you card to a friend or family member for their support. (h) Go to the library (do a web walk) to look something up out of interest, not for an assignment.

How to enhance performance. Athletes, actors and other performers have techniques to enhance their performance that can be used for other activities. These techniques include (a) relaxed visualization of successfully completing the task, (b) positive self-talk about the ability to succeed and (c) cognitive restructuring in which failure is attributed to something you can do something about (e.g., poor preparation).

Level 4: Integrate Knowledge and Procedures
Execute plans, Solve problems

Integrating personal excellence and hard work. Students add to their areas of excellence, always trying to apply it in all areas. Have students work with a mentor in areas they want to maintain or improve.

Wise decision making. Discuss the tenets of wisdom. Discuss how keeping them in mind might affect your decision making.

Apply wisdom in everyday life. Students exhibit the tenets of wisdom through journaling about their community service experiences and reflecting on the tenets of wisdom.

Survey your internal and external assets. Have students go to the Search Institute's web site and take the 40-asset survey (or print and hand out): http://www.search-institute.org/assets/forty.htm. Have students create a plan to increase their assets. Set up a strategic plan with specific goals. Rank order the assets you need. Design steps to increase each asset. Make the steps small enough so that success is apparent. Set a timeline for taking the steps and get started. The class members should support each other in these efforts (perhaps in pairs or small groups). Once they get going they can help younger students build assets too.

Starred ★ activities within each subskill go together!

Working Hard
by Taking Charge of Your Life
Ideas for Developing Skills

Level 4 (continued)

Making a strategic plan to create your dreams (adapted from McGraw, 2000). Write down 5 dreams you have for your life. Take one dream and make a strategic plan: (a) What does reaching this dream look like in terms of concrete behaviors? (b) What are the specific goals that go with the dream and how will I know I have reached the goals? (c) What is the difference between where I want to go and where I am today? (d) For one of the goals, what are the steps I need to take to get to where I want to go? (e) What is my timeline for reaching each step? (f) How can I break down each step into doable chunks? (g) What can I do now to start working towards completing a step? Have students begin their path towards meeting their steps, goals and dreams. Have them keep track of their progress in a diary. The class members should give each other support during this process.

Assessment Hints

Working for Excellence

Have students write reports, based on observations or interviews, of how others worked hard to achieve excellence; students can present their reports to the class.

Present a written scenario or video clip of hard work (or lack of hard work) and have students respond in writing.

Use a real-life biography of someone who worked hard and have students describe the behaviors of the person.

Have students keep a journal of their own reflections of what they would like to work hard in, what they have worked hard on recently, and when they should have worked harder than they did; assess the journal entries.

Have students write essays, poems, songs, music, or plays about taking charge of their life.

Have students create and participate in social action projects such as petitions, demonstrations, letter writing, advocacy, campaigning.

Create a Cimate
to Develop Working Hard

In order for students to develop their minds and selves, they need to have goals that are just beyond their reach but attainable with effort.
- Help students identify their own goals for themselves in school and beyond. This can be done on a weekly or monthly basis.
- Let students participate in setting high standards for the class.

Foster these attitudes:
- Working hard to help others makes the world a better place for everyone.
- Community involvement is important everyone.
- It is important to set high standards for myself in terms of amount of work and quality of work.
- It is important for the teacher to set high standards for me and for the class in terms of amount of work and quality of work.
- People are the happiest when they have work they love and relationships they appreciate.
- Some people have to work hard and endure boring and tedious journeys to attain the kind of work they love.

Selections to Post in the Classroom
for Working Hard

WISDOM

Wisdom is the chief aspect of a complex self. Wisdom does not succumb to the superficial aspect of things but searches for the enduring truths that lie below them.

From *The Tenets of Wisdom* (Csikszentmihalyi, 1993, pp. 289-290):
1. *You are a part of everything around you: the air, the earth and the sea; the past and the future.* If you bring disorder to any of these, you bring harm upon your own self as well.
2. *You shall not deny your uniqueness.* You are the only center of consciousness in your space-time location.
3. *You are responsible for your actions.* If you achieve control over your minds, your desires, and your actions, you are likely to increase order around you.
4. *You shall be more than what you are.* The self is a creative construction. No one is ever complete and finished.

Sample Student Self-Monitoring
Working Hard

Encourage active learning by having students learn to monitor their own learning

Set reachable goals

When I play a game, I like to play with someone who is a little better than me.

Manage Time

I know what to do to manage my time.
I manage my time as a way to take control of my life.
I practice time management.

Take Charge of Your Life

I like challenges.
I like to work hard at solving problems.
I like to figure things out myself.
I like it best when things are not too easy to do.
I know ways to take charge of my life.
I am making choices that affect my future.
I look forward to the future.

Selections to Post in the Classroom
for Working Hard

AVOID THESE TIME WASTERS

Attempting to do too much at once
Unrealistic expectations
Lack of specific priorities
Failure to listen well
Unable to say no
Perfectionism—caught up in unimportant detail
Lack of organization
Failure to write it down
Reluctance to get started
Absence of self-appointed deadlines
Doing everything yourself when you could delegate some things

Ethical Action Appendix

Lesson Planning Guide

'Linking to the Community' Worksheet

Rubric Examples
    Journaling
    Papers or Reports

Special Activities
    Cognitive Apprenticeship
    Cooperative Learning
    Guidelines for Cross-Age Tutoring
    Reciprocal Teaching
    The Jigsaw Method
    Structured Controversy

Making a Strategic Plan for Change

Linking EA Skills to Search Institute Assets

Recommended Resources for Character Education

Resources/References for Ethical Action
    Maslow's Hierarchy of Needs
    Conflict Resolution Education Network (CREnet)
    References Cited in Booklet

Lesson Planning Guide

1. **Select an ethical category and identify the subskill you will address in your lesson(s).**

2. **Select a graduation standard or academic requirement and identify the sub-components.**

3. **Match up the ethical sub-skill with the academic sub-components.**

4. **Generate lesson activities using these elements:**

   (a) Enlist the communities resources.
   (For ideas, consult the Linking to Community worksheet, pp. 134-139)

   (b) Focus on a variety of teaching styles and intelligences.
   Teaching styles: Visual, Auditory, Tactile, Kinesthetic, Oral, Individual/Cooperative, Olfactory, Gustatory, Spatial

   Intelligences: Musical, Bodily-Kinesthetic, Spatial Logico-Mathematical, Linguistic, Interpersonal, Intrapersonal

   (c) Identify questions that you can ask that promote different kinds of thinking and memory.

   Creative Thinking

   Prospective Thinking

   Retrospective Thinking

   Motivational Thinking

   Practical Thinking

   Types of Memory:

   > Autobiographical (personal experience)

   > Narrative (storyline)

   > Procedural (how to)

   > Semantic (what)

5. **Create an activity for each <u>level of expertise</u> you will address (worksheet provided on next page). Indicate which activities fit with which lesson. For each activity, indicate how you will <u>assess learning</u>.**

Lesson Planning Guide
(continued)

<u>ACTIVITY</u>   <u>STUDENT ASSESSMENT</u>

Level 1: Immersion in Examples and Opportunities
(Attend to the big picture, Learn to recognize basic patterns)

Level 2: Attention to Facts and Skills
(Focus on detail and prototypical examples, Build knowledge)

Level 3: Practice Procedures
(Set goals, Plan steps of problem solving, Practice skills)

Level 4: Integrate Knowledge and Procedures
(Execute plans, Solve problems)

Ethical Action Appendix

CHECKLIST FOR
Linking to the Community

What resources must be accessed for learning the skill or subskill?

What resources must be identified to successfully complete the skill or subskill?

1. SOCIAL NETWORK RESOURCES

Circle the resources that must be accessed for learning the skill:

Family____   Friendship____   Service group____

Neighborhood____   Social groups ____   Community____

City____   Park & Rec____   State____

National ____   International____

Other:_____Other:_____

On the line next to each circled item, indicate the <u>manner of contact</u>:

Contact in person (P), by telephone (T)

2. SEMANTIC KNOWLEDGE RESOURCES

Circle the resources that must be accessed for learning the skill:

Books and other library sources____   Web____

Librarians____   Educators and Intellectuals____

Business leaders____   Community experts____

Other:_____   Other:_____

On the line next to each circled item, indicate the <u>manner of contact</u>:

Contact in person (P), Email (E), Web (W), Letter (L), Telephone (T)

CHECKLIST FOR
Linking to the Community
(continued)

3. AUTHORITY STRUCTURE RESOURCES

Circle the resources that must be accessed for learning the skill:

School officials____   Government officials (all levels) ____ United Nations____

Other Leaders:_____

_____

_____

Indicate the manner of contact for each item:

Contact in person (P), Telephone (T), Letter (L), Email (E)

4. ORGANIZATIONAL RESOURCES

What types of organizations can give guidance?

_____

_____

_____

_____

How can they help?

_____

_____

_____

_____

_____

_____

_____

_____

_____

Ethical Action Appendix

Ethical Action Appendix

5. AGE GROUP RESOURCES

Circle the resources that must be accessed for learning the skill:

- Teen groups in various community organizations_____

    Specify:

- School groups_____

    Specify:

- Senior citizen groups_____

    Specify:

- Children's groups_____

    Specify:

- Women's groups_____

    Specify:

- Men's groups_____

    Specify:

Indicate the manner of contact for each circled item:

Contact in person (P), Telephone (T), Letter (L), Email (E)

CHECKLIST FOR
Linking to the Community
(continued)

6. MATERIAL RESOURCES

<u>Types of Materials</u>

* scraps (from scrap yards)

* second-hand (from second-hand stores, recycling places)

* new

* handmade

Identify the resources that must be accessed for learning the skill:

What materials do you need for your project?

_____

_____

_____

Where can you get it?

_____

_____

_____

How can you get it?

_____

_____

_____

Indicate the manner of contact for each item:

Contact in person (P), Telephone (T), Letter (L), Email (E)

7. EXPERTISE RESOURCES

Types of Expertise

social networking_____   design _____   musical _____

physical (game/sport, dance)_____ creating_____   knowledge _____

finance_____   selling_____

Identify the resources that must be accessed for learning the skill:

What expertise is required?

_____

_____

_____

_____

Who has expertise?

_____

_____

_____

Can I develop expertise or must I depend on an expert?

_____

_____

Who can help me figure out what to do?

_____

_____

_____

Indicate the manner of contact for each item:

Telephone (T), Take a class (C), Contact in person (P), Book (B)

CHECKLIST FOR
Linking to the Community
(continued)

8. FINANCIAL RESOURCES

Circle the sources that must be accessed for learning the skill:

Grants____   Loans____   Donors____

Earn money____

Bartering (use library and experts to find these out) ____

Indicate the manner of contact for each circled item:

Contact in person (P), Telephone (T), Email (E), Letter (L)

9. PERSONAL RESOURCES

What abilities and skills do I have that I can use to reach the goal?

_____

_____

_____

_____

10. OTHER RESOURCES

What other resources might be needed or are optional?

_____

_____

_____

_____

Rubric Examples

GUIDES FOR CREATING YOUR OWN RUBRIC

> **Creating Rubrics**
> (Blueprint of behavior for peak or acceptable level of performance)
>
> ❖ Establish Learner Outcome goals
> ❖ Cluster these characteristics
> ❖ Determine which combinations of characteristics show
>   Unsatisfactory, Satisfactory, Excellent 'job'
> ❖ Create examples of work showing different levels of performance
> ❖ List expectations on a form
> ❖ Present criteria to students ahead of time

RUBRIC FOR JOURNALING

Quality of Journaling		
Content: Quantity Few requirements for content are covered. 0 1 2 3	Most requirements are included fairly well. 4 5 6 7	Content requirements are thoroughly covered. 8 9 10
Content: Type Rarely are both feelings and thoughts included in entries. 0 1 2 3	Sometimes both feelings and thoughts are included in entries. 4 5 6 7	Both feelings and thoughts are included in entries. 8 9 10
Content: Clarity Entries are difficult to understand. 0 1 2 3	Entries can be understood with some effort. 4 5 6 7	Entries are easily understood. 8 9 10

Rubric Examples (continued)

RUBRIC FOR PAPERS OR REPORTS

Qualities of Paper or Written Report		
Organization The paper is difficult to follow. 0 1 2 3	The paper is easy to follow and read. 4 5 6 7	All relationships among ideas are clearly expressed by the sentence structures and word choices. 8 9 10
Writing Style The style of the writing is sloppy, has no clear direction, looks like it was written by several people. 0 1 2 3	The format is appropriate with correct spelling, good grammar, good punctuation and appropriate transition sentences. 4 5 6 7	The paper is well written and is appropriate for presentation in the firm. 8 9 10
Content The paper has no point. The ideas are aimless, disconnected. 0 1 2 3	The paper makes a couple of clear points but weakly, with few supportive facts. 4 5 6 7	The paper makes one or two strong points. Support for these arguments is well described. 8 9 10

Ethical Action Appendix

Special Activities

COGNITIVE APPRENTICESHIP
(Collins, Hawkins, & Carver, 1991, p. 228)

Teach *process* (how to) and *provide guided experience* in cognitive skills.

Teach *content* relevant to the task.

Teach this content for each subject area:

> Strategic knowledge: how to work successfully in the subject area
>
> Domain knowledge: the kind of knowledge experts know
>
> Problem solving strategies particular to the subject area

Learning strategies for the subject area

Teaching methods to use:

> Expert modeling
>
> Coaching
>
> Scaffolding (lots of structured assistance at first, gradual withdrawal of support)
>
> Articulation by students
>
> Reflection
>
> Exploration

How to sequence material:

> Increasing complexity
>
> Increasing diversity
>
> Global (the big picture) before the local (the detail)

Learning environment should emphasize:

> Situated learning
>
> Community of practice
>
> Intrinsic motivation
>
> Cooperation

COOPERATIVE LEARNING

Necessary elements in using cooperative learning to improve role-taking (Bridgeman, 1981)

1. Required interdependence and social reciprocity
2. Consistent opportunity to be an expert
3. Integration of varied perspectives and appreciation for the result
4. Equal status cooperation
5. Highly structured to allow easy replication of these interactions

Special Activities

GUILDELINES FOR CROSS-GRADE TUTORING

(Heath & Mangiola, 1991)

1. Allow a preparation period of at least 1 month to 6 weeks for the student tutors.

2. Use as much writing as possible in the context of the tutoring from the very beginning. Use a variety of sources and use the tutoring as a basis for tutors to write to different audiences.

3. Make field notes meaningful as a basis for conversation by providing students with occasions to share their notes orally.

4. Provide students with supportive models of open-ended questioning.

5. Emphasize the ways in which tutors can extend tutees' responses and elicit elaboration from tutees in order to impress upon them the importance of talk in learning.

6. Discuss the ways the topic relates to students' experiences.

7. Provide opportunities for tutors to prepare.

8. Develop real audiences for the students' work.

RECIPROCAL TEACHING (RT)

Context	One-on-one in laboratory settings	Groups in resource rooms	Naturally occurring groups in classrooms	Work groups fully integrated into science classrooms
Activities	Summarizing, questioning, clarifying, predicting	Gist and analogy	Complex argument structure	Thought experiments
Materials	Unconnected passages	Coherent content	Research-related resources material	Student-prepared
Pattern of use	Individual strategy training	Group discussion	Planned RT for learning content and jigsaw teaching	Opportunistic use of RT

Ethical Action Appendix

Special Activities

THE JIGSAW METHOD
(Aronson & Patnoe, 1997)

The Jigsaw Method of cooperative learning helps children work together on an equal basis. It has been shown to improve empathy for fellow students, mastery of course material, liking of school and liking of classmates.

Goal: That students treat each other as resources
Instructional outcome: Students learn that it is possible to work together without sacrificing excellence.
Structure:

      Individual competition is incompatible with success

      Success is dependent on cooperative behavior

      All students has unique information to bring to the group.

You must provide material written by relative experts. This could be an article broken into pieces or could be cards on which you write critical information.

1. Divide the written material into 3-6 coherent parts (could be by paragraphs).
2. Assign students to 3-5 groups.
3. Assign one part of the material to each group member.
4. Those with the same part meet in groups to learn their knowledge (10-15 minutes).
5. Group members return to their original groups to learn from their group.
6. Everyone takes a quiz on all the material.

STRUCTURED CONTROVERSY

The steps for a structured academic controversy (Johnson & Johnson, 1997) are as follows:

(1) Select an issue relevant to what you are studying. Select two or more opinions on the issue.

(2) Form advocacy teams by putting the students into groups for each different opinion. Either put together a list of supporting statements for each opinion, or have students research the opinion and come up with their own supporting statements (if this is done, provide guidance and feedback for the accuracy and comprehensiveness of the supporting statements they generate). Each group prepares a persuasive statement based on the supporting statements of their opinion.

(3) Have each group present its persuasive case to the other groups without interruption. Students in the listening groups should listen carefully and take notes to learn the other opinion well.

(4) Have open discussion among the groups with advocacy of their own position and refutation of other positions (respectfully).

(5) Groups trade positions on the issue to take another group's perspective. The group must present the other perspective to the others as sincerely and persuasively as the original group did. The group can add new facts, information, or arguments to the position (based on what they have already learned) to make it more persuasive.

(6) All individuals drop their advocacy and group-orientation to discuss the positions again and try to come to a consensus about which position is the best. The position can be one that is a synthesis of two or more, as long as the position isn't a simple compromise.

Special Activities

STRUCTURED CONTROVERSY
LESSON PLANNING SHEET

Grade Level_____   Subject area_____

Size of group_____   How groups formed_____

Room arrangement_____

Issue_____

     One perspective_____

     Second perspective_____

     Third perspective_____

Student materials required_____

Define the controversy_____

_____

_____

Making a strategic plan for change

1. **What I/we want to change:**

2. **The end result I/we want:**

3. **What is current reality—now?** Identify the difference between where things stand now and where you want to get to.

4. **What steps do I/we need to take to get to the desired end result?** Brainstorm on methods or strategies to reach your objectives. Don't eliminate any methods or strategies at this point.

5. **How will I/we know my/our actions are working?** Brainstorm on ways to check that actions are or are not working.

6. **Now select the best goals and the best set of steps to reach them.** Make sure:
- That the goals are going to reach the end result we desire. (Imagine the strategies successfully completed.)
- To quantify the goal where you can.
- To translate comparative terms (e.g., more, better, less, increased) into their actual goals.
- To create long-term, lasting results rather than just solving individual problems.
- That your goals describe an actual result rather than only a process for achieving that result.
- That your goals are specific.

Linking EA Skills to Search Institute Assets

VIRTUE / SUBSKILL	EA-1 Resolving Conflicts	EA-2 Learning Persuasion	EA-3 Initiative as Leader	EA-4 Planning	EA-5 Cultivating Courage	EA-6 Persevering	EA-7 Working Hard
1. Family support							
2. Positive family comm.	*						
3. Other adult relationships							
4. Caring neighborhood							
5. Caring school climate							
6. Parent involvement in school							
7. Community values youth							
8. Youth as resources		*		*			
9. Service to others			*				
10. Safety		*					
11. Family boundaries							
12. School boundaries							
13. Neighborhood boundaries							
14. Adult role models							
15. Positive peer influence		*					
16. High expectations							
17. Creative activities							
18. Youth programs							
19. Religious community							
20. Time at home							
21. Achievement motivation							
22. School engagement				*		*	
23. Homework							
24. Bonding to school							
25. Reading for pleasure							
26. Caring	*						
27. Equality and social justice			*		*		
28. Integrity			*		*		
29. Honesty							
30. Responsibility			*		*		
31. Restraint				*		*	
32. Planning and decision making			*	*			
33. Interpersonal competence	*	*	*				
34. Cultural competence							
35. Resistance skills	*	*				*	
36. Peaceful conflict resolution	*						
37. Personal power		*	*		*		*
38. Self-esteem							*
39. Sense of purpose					*		*
40. Positive view of personal future							*

Recommended Resources
for Character Education

De Vries, R., & Zan, B. S. (1994). *Moral classrooms, moral children: Creating a constructivist atmosphere in early education.* New York: Teachers College Press.

Elias, M. J., Arnold, H., & Hussey, C. S. (Eds.). (2002). *EQ + IQ = Best leadership practices for caring and successful schools.* Thousand Oaks, CA: Corwin Press

Gootman, M. E. (2008). *The caring teacher's guide to discipline: Helping students learn self-control, responsibility, and respect, K-6* (3rd ed.). Thousand Oaks, CA: Corwin Press.

Greene, A. (1996). *Rights to responsibility: Multiple approaches to developing character and community.* Tucson, AZ: Zephyr.

Jweid, R., & Rizzo, M. (2001). *Building character through literature: A guide for middle school readers.* Lanham, MD: Scarecrow.

Kirschenbaum, H. (1994). *100 ways to enhance values and morality in schools and youth meetings.* Boston: Allyn & Bacon.

Lantieri, L., & Goleman, D. (2008). *Building emotional intelligence: Techniques to cultivate inner strength in children.* Boulder, CO: Sounds True, Incorporated.

Liebling, C. R. (1986). *Inside view and character plans in original stories and their basal reader adaptations.* Washington, DC: National Institute of Education.

Miller, J. C., & Clarke, C. (1998). *10-minute life lessons for kids: 52 fun and simple games and activities to teach your child trust, honesty, love, and other important values.* New York: HarperPerennial Library.

Nucci, L. P., & Narvaez, D. (Eds.). (2008). *Handbook of moral and character education.* New York: Routledge.

Power, F. C., Nuzzi, R. J., Narvaez, D., Lapsley, D. K., & Hunt, T. C. (Eds.). (2008). *Moral education: A handbook* (Vols. 1-2). Westport, CT: Praeger.

Ryan, K. A., & Bohlin, K. E. (2000). *Building character in schools: Practical ways to bring moral instruction to life.* San Francisco: Jossey-Bass.

Ryan, K., & Wynne, E. A. (1996). *Reclaiming our schools: Teaching character, academics, and discipline.* Upper Saddle River, NJ: Prentice Hall.

Watson, M., & Eckert, L. (2003). *Learning to trust.* San Francisco: Jossey-Bass.

Ethical Action Appendix

Resources/References for Ethical Action

Maslow's (1943) Hierarchy of Basic Needs

These usually must be satisfied in order (e.g., need satisfaction of safety needs before manifesting a need for esteem)

(1) Physiological Needs (e.g., rest, food, drink, warmth, exercise, stimulation)

(2) Safety Needs (e.g., security, stability, dependency, protection, freedom from fear and chaos, structure/order/law/limits)

(3) Belongingness Needs (e.g., giving and receiving: love, affection, friendship; group solidarity)

(4) Esteem Needs

    a. Achievement, mastery, competence, confidence

    b. Reputation, status, appreciation, importance, dignity

(5) Self-actualization (e.g., self-fulfillment, reaching one's potential)

Conflict Resolution Information Source
c/o Conflict Information Consortium
University of Colorado
Campus Box 580
Boulder CO 80309
www.crinfo.org/
Description: A clearinghouse for information, resources, and technical assistance in the field of conflict resolution education.

References for Ethical Action

Alberti, R. E., & Emmons, M. L. (1974). *Your perfect right*. San Luis Obispo, CA: Impact.

Alberti, R. E., & Emmons, M. L. (1975). *Stand up, speak out, talk back!* New York: Pocket Books.

Aronson, E., & Patnoe, S. (1997). *The jigsaw classroom: Building cooperation in the classroom.* New York: Longman.

Baltes, P., & Straudinger, U. M. (2000). Wisdom: A metheuristic (pragmatic) to orchestrate mind and virtue toward excellence. *American Psychologist, 55*(1), 122-136.

Benard, B. (1995). *Fostering resilience in children.* Urbana, IL: ERIC Clearinghouse on Elementary and Early Childhood Education, University of Illinois.

Berman, S. (1997). *Children's social consciousness and the development of social responsibility.* Albany: State University of New York Press.

Borba, M. (1999). *Building moral intelligence: The seven essential virtues that teach kids to do the right thing.* New York: Jossey-Bass.

Bridgeman, D. (1981). Enhanced role-taking through cooperative interdependence: A field study. *Child Development, 52*, 1231-1238.

Carson, R. (1962). *Silent spring.* Boston: Houghton Mifflin.

Cianciosi, J. (2001). *The meditative path.* New York: Quest.

Collins, A., Hawkins, J., & Carver, S. M. (1991). A cognitive apprenticeship for disadvantaged students.In B. Means, C. Chelemer, M. S. Knapp (Eds.), *Teaching advanced skills to at-risk students* (pp. 216-243). San Francisco, Jossey-Bass.

Csikszentmihalyi, M. (1993). *The evolving self.* New York: HarperCollins.

Dotson, A., & Dotson, K. (1997). *Teaching character: Teacher's idea book.* Chapel Hill, NC: Character Development Group.

Douglass, F. (1960). *Narrative of the life of Frederick Douglass: An American slave.* Cambridge, MA: Belknap Press.

Eisenberg, N., & Mussen, P. H. (1989). *The roots of prosocial behavior in children.* Cambridge, MA: Cambridge University Press.

Enright, R. (2001). *Forgiveness is a choice: A step-by-step process for resolving anger and restoring hope.* Washington, DC: American Psychological Association.

Fisher, R., Ury, W., & Patton, B. (1991). *Getting to yes: Negotiating agreement without giving in.* London: Penguin.

Forni, P. M. (2001). *Choosing civility: The twenty-five rules of considerate conduct.* New York: St. Martin's Griffin.

Frankel, F. H. (1996). *Good friends are hard to find: Help your child find, make, and keep friends.* Los Angeles, CA: Perspective Publications.

Friel, J. C., & Friel, L. D. (2000). *The 7 best things (smart) teens do.* Deerfield Beach, FL: Health Communications.

Gibbs, J., Potter, G., & Goldstein, A. (1995). *The EQUIP Program: Teaching youth to think and act responsibly through a peer-helping approach.* Champaign, IL: Research Press.

Gladwell, M. (2002). *The tipping point: How little things can make a big difference.* Boston: Little, Brown.

References for Ethical Action

(continued)

Greer, C., & Kohl, E. R. (Eds.). (1995). *A call to character: A family treasure of stories, poems, plays, proverbs, and fables to guide the development of values for and your children.* New York: HarperCollins Publishers.

Heath, S. B., & Mangiola, L. (1991). *Children of promise: Literate activity in linguistically and culturally diverse classrooms.* Washington, DC: National Education Association.

Johnson, D. W. (1993). *Reaching out.* New York: Allyn & Bacon.

Johnson, D. W., & Johnson, F. (1997). *Joining together: Group theory and group skills* (6th ed.). Boston: Allyn & Bacon.

Kurtzman, L. (1998, October). *Peer leaders: Cross-age Grade 7 and 6 to Grade 4 and 3.* Paper presented at the meeting of the Character Education Partnership, Denver, CO.

Lewis, B. A., Espeland, P., & Pernu, C. (1998). *The kid's guide to social action: How to solve the social problems you choose and turn creative thinking into positive action.* Minneapolis, MN: Freespirit.

Lickona, T. (1991). *Educating for character: How our schools can teach respect and responsibility.* New York: Bantam.

Lufi, D., & Cohen, A. (1987). A scale for measuring persistence in children. *Journal of Personality Assessment, 51,* 178-185.

Marzano, R.J. (2003). *What works in schools.* Alexandria, VA: Association for Supervision and Curriculum.

Maslow, A. (1943). A theory of human motivation. *Psychological Review, 50*(4), 370-396.

Maier, N. R. F. (1963). *Problem-solving discussions and conferences.* New York: McGraw-Hill.

McGraw, J. (2000). *Life strategies for teens.* New York: Fireside.

Paul, R. (1987). *Critical thinking handbook, 4th-6th grades: A guide for remodeling lesson plans in language arts, social studies, and science.* Rohnert Park, CA: Center for Critical Thinking and Moral Critique.

Pratkanis, A. R., & Aronson, E. (1992). *Age of propaganda: The everyday use and abuse of persuasion.* New York: W. H. Freeman.

Prothrow-Stith, D., & Weissman, M. (1991). *Deadly consequences: How violence is destroying our teenage population and a plan to begin solving the problem.* New York: Harper Perennial.

Seligman, M. (1995). *The optimistic child.* New York: HarperCollins.

Sisk, D., & Rosselli, H. (1987). *Leadership: A special type of giftedness.* Monroe, NY: Trillium Press.

Sowell, T. (1994). *Race and culture.* New York: Basic Books.

Sowell, T. (1996). *Migration and cultures.* New York: Basic Books.

Tan, A. (1989). *The joy luck club.* New York: Putnam.

Turner, M. E., & Pratkanis, A. R. (1994). *Social psychological perspectives on affirmative action.* Hillsdale, NJ: Lawrence Erlbaum Associates.

Zimmerman, B. J., Bonner, S., & Kovach, R. (2002). *Developing self-regulated learners.* Washington, DC: American Psychological Association.

Ethical Action Appendix

About the Author

Darcia Narvaez, Ph.D., Associate Professor of Psychology at the University of Notre Dame, developed the Integrative Ethical Education model (initiated under the federally-funded Minnesota Community Voices and Character Education Project which she reported on at a Whitehouse conference). Previously at the University of Minnesota, she was executive director of the Center for the Study of Ethical Development and was director of the Center for Ethical Education at the University of Notre Dame. She is on the editorial boards of the *Journal of Educational Psychology* and the *Journal of Moral Education*. She has published in the *Journal of Educational Psychology, Developmental Psychology*, and has two award-winning books, *Postconventional Moral Thinking* (1999; with Rest, Bebeau & Thoma) and *Moral Development, Self and Identity* (2004; with Lapsley).

www.ingramcontent.com/pod-product-compliance
Lightning Source LLC
Chambersburg PA
CBHW081150090426
42736CB00017B/3257